MW01005927

THE RELIGION CLAUSES

David A. Strauss
GERALD RATNER DISTINGUISHED SERVICE
PROFESSOR OF LAW
UNIVERSITY OF CHICAGO LAW SCHOOL

Kathleen M. Sullivan
STANLEY MORRISON PROFESSOR OF LAW
STANFORD LAW SCHOOL

Cass R. Sunstein
ROBERT WALMSLEY UNIVERSITY PROFESSOR
HARVARD LAW SCHOOL

Laurence H. Tribe
CARL M. LOEB UNIVERSITY
PROFESSOR OF LAW
HARVARD LAW SCHOOL

Mark V. Tushnet
WILLIAM NELSON CROMWELL
PROFESSOR OF LAW
HARVARD LAW SCHOOL

J. Harvie Wilkinson III
JUDGE
US COURT OF APPEALS FOR
THE FOURTH CIRCUIT

Kenji Yoshino
CHIEF JUSTICE EARL
WARREN PROFESSOR OF
CONSTITUTIONAL LAW
NEW YORK UNIVERSITY
SCHOOL OF LAW

GEOFFREY STONE AND OXFORD UNIVERSITY PRESS GRATEFULLY ACKNOWLEDGE THE INTEREST AND SUPPORT OF THE FOLLOWING ORGANIZATIONS IN THE INALIENABLE RIGHTS SERIES: THE ALA; THE CHICAGO HUMANITIES FESTIVAL; THE AMERICAN BAR ASSOCIATION; THE NATIONAL CONSTITUTION CENTER; THE NATIONAL ARCHIVES

The Religion Clauses

The Case for Separating Church and State

Howard Gillman and Erwin Chemerinsky

OXFORD
UNIVERSITY PRESS

OXFORD
UNIVERSITY PRESS

Oxford University Press is a department of the University of Oxford. It furthers
the University's objective of excellence in research, scholarship, and education
by publishing worldwide. Oxford is a registered trade mark of Oxford University
Press in the UK and certain other countries.

Published in the United States of America by Oxford University Press
198 Madison Avenue, New York, NY 10016, United States of America.

Library of Congress Cataloging-in-Publication Data
Names: Gillman, Howard, author. | Chemerinsky, Erwin, author.
Title: The religion clauses: the case for separating church and state /
Howard Gillman, Erwin Chemerinsky.
Description: New York : Oxford University Press, 2020. |
Series: Inalienable Rights Series | Includes index. |
Identifiers: LCCN 2019052833 | ISBN 9780190699734 (hardback) |
ISBN 9780190699758 (epub)
Subjects: LCSH: Church and state—United States. |
Freedom of religion—United States.
Classification: LCC KF4865 .C486 2020 | DDC 342.7308/52—dc23
LC record available at https://lccn.loc.gov/2019052833

1 3 5 7 9 8 6 4 2
Printed by LSC Communications, United States of America

Contents

. . .

Preface

. . .

The United States Supreme Court appears to be on the verge of major shifts in interpreting the Religion Clauses of the First Amendment. The five conservative justices—John Roberts, Clarence Thomas, Samuel Alito, Neil Gorsuch, and Brett Kavanaugh—reject the idea of a wall separating church and state. They believe that the Establishment Clause—the provision of the First Amendment prohibiting any law respecting the establishment of religion—should be interpreted to accommodate religious participation in government and government support for religious institutions.[1] Under their view, the government violates the Establishment Clause only if it coerces religious participation or discriminates among religions in the provision of benefits. Under this approach, the Establishment Clause is not violated by religious symbols on government property,[2] or by religious observances at government functions,[3] or by the government providing financial support to religious institutions even when the money is used for religious indoctrination.[4]

At the same time, the conservative members of the Court seem poised to interpret the Free Exercise Clause—the provision of the

First Amendment prohibiting the government from abridging free exercise of religion—as requiring that the government accommodate religious beliefs by granting exceptions to general laws. For example, in *Burwell v. Hobby Lobby*, the Court held, 5–4, that it violates the Religious Freedom Restoration Act to require that a large family-owned business provide insurance coverage for contraceptives for women when that violates the business owners' religious beliefs.[5] The five conservative justices then on the Court concluded that it violates religious freedom for federal law to require a corporation to provide women employees coverage for contraceptives if doing so would violate the business owner's religious beliefs. Although it is not resolved, there well may be five votes on the current Court to hold that it violates free exercise of religion (and/or freedom of speech) to force a business owner to provide services to a same-sex wedding when that offends the business owner's religious beliefs.[6] Under this accommodationist view, the Free Exercise Clause will be interpreted to require religious exemptions from federal, state, and local laws, including and especially civil rights laws.

At the same time, the five conservative justices seem ready to hold that the government is constitutionally *required* to provide benefits to religious institutions whenever it gives them to secular private institutions. In *Trinity Lutheran Church of Columbia v. Comer*,[7] in 2017, the Supreme Court held that Missouri violated the Free Exercise Clause of the First Amendment by denying a church an otherwise available public benefit—assistance for surfacing playgrounds—on account of its religious status. Chief Justice Roberts wrote for the Court and said that Missouri was discriminating against religious institutions in the receipt of this benefit and that therefore the state had to meet strict scrutiny—showing that its action was necessary to achieve a compelling government purpose—under the Free Exercise Clause to justify the denial of the benefit. The Court declared: "Trinity Lutheran is a member of the community too, and the State's decision to exclude it for purposes of this public program must withstand the strictest scrutiny."[8]

We write this book to describe and critique where the Court appears to be going but also to advance an alternative vision of the Religion Clauses of the First Amendment. In contrast to the accommodationist approach of the Court's majority, we defend a separationist view. The Establishment Clause should be interpreted, to the greatest extent practical, to require separation of church and state. Under this view, the government should be secular; the place for religion is in people's lives, their homes, and their places of worship.

Free exercise of religion protects the right of people to believe what they wish and to practice their religions however they choose, but it does not provide a basis for people to harm others based on their religious beliefs or for an exception from general laws. Under our separationist view, religion does not provide a basis for employers to deny contraceptive coverage to their employees or businesses to discriminate against same-sex couples.

Although we are not originalists and do not believe that the meaning of a constitutional provision is determined by the original understanding at the time it was adopted (even assuming that could be known), we think that history and context are important in understanding the current issues with regard to the Religion Clauses of the First Amendment. We are convinced, as we argue in Chapter 2, that those who drafted the Constitution, including the Bill of Rights, overwhelmingly wanted a secular government and separation in the way we describe for both the Establishment Clause and the Free Exercise Clause.

We think it important at the outset to look at the political context in which these issues arise and come to the Supreme Court. As we explain in Chapter 1, over the last few decades, and especially since the Ronald Reagan campaign in 1980, the Republican political strategy has been to appeal to and rely on white Christian voters.

Republicans have appealed to this group by denouncing abortion rights and also by taking positions on the Religion Clauses (and other political issues) likely to appeal to Christians. It is not surprising then that the conservative judicial ideology has followed the position of conservative political candidates.

Virtually every recent Supreme Court case about the Religion Clauses has involved whether the government can accommodate Christianity. For instance, in *Town of Greece v. Galloway* (2014), the Court held that it does not violate the Establishment Clause for a town board to begin virtually every meeting with a prayer, as it has done for ten years—and usually a very explicit Christian prayer by a Christian minister.[9] In *Burwell v. Hobby Lobby* (2014), the Court said that business owners could refuse to provide contraceptive coverage because they had sincere Christian beliefs that life begins at conception and that it would violate their religion to facilitate access to contraceptive drugs or devices that operate after that point.[10] In *Trinity Lutheran Church of Columbia v. Comer* (2017), the Court found that it violated free exercise of religion to deny a Christian school benefits that it provides to secular private schools.[11]

We find it hard to reconcile that when it was a non-Christian religion suffering discrimination, the five most conservative justices rejected a challenge based on the Religion Clauses. In *Trump v. Hawaii* (2018), the Court upheld President Trump's travel ban even though he repeatedly declared that his goal was to prevent Muslims from entering the country.[12] As Justice Sotomayor pointed out in dissent, "The full record paints a far more harrowing picture, from which a reasonable observer would readily conclude that the Proclamation was motivated by hostility and animus toward the Muslim faith."[13] In fact, the key case narrowing the protections for the Free Exercise Clause, *Employment Division v. Smith* (1990), rejected religious freedom claims by Native Americans.[14]

In other words, whether self-consciously or not, the five conservative justices are interpreting the Constitution to further Christian religious beliefs, finding that the government does not violate the Establishment Clause if it acts to further Christianity and that it must, based on free exercise of religion, accommodate Christians who want exceptions from general laws, such as those requiring that employers provide contraceptive coverage or prohibiting discrimination against gays and lesbians.[15] The most vocal and politically powerful groups advocating closer ties between the government and religion also arise from more conservative Christian sects.[16] Sympathetic politicians at the national and state level who support accommodationist policies focus almost exclusively on Christian religious freedom, with an emphasis on Christian religious imagery on public property and allowing people to refuse to serve the lesbian, gay, bisexual, transgender, and questioning (or queer) (LGBTQ) community.[17]

We argue for a different vision: one that seeks to separate government and religion, both with regard to the Establishment Clause and the Free Exercise Clause. As we explain, we believe that this is consistent with the views of those who drafted the Constitution, is supported by the lessons of history, and most important, is the best way to interpret the Religion Clauses for a society that is increasingly religiously diverse.

CHAPTER ONE

The Competing Perspectives of the Religion Clauses

RECENT CASES

THE FIRST AMENDMENT begins with the words: "Congress shall make no law respecting an establishment of religion, or prohibiting the free exercise thereof." These two clauses are commonly referred to, respectively, as the "Establishment Clause" and the "Free Exercise Clause."

Over the last several years, the Supreme Court has considered a number of highly controversial cases concerning these provisions. The decisions reveal a great deal about the deep division in our society concerning the appropriate role of government and religion. They also give a sense of the direction of the current Supreme Court and how it is going to treat the Religion Clauses for the foreseeable future. Consider several examples:

- At issue in *Burwell v. Hobby Lobby* (2014)[1] was a federal statute that required employer health insurance to include preventative health care coverage for women, including contraceptive coverage. Although religious institutions and nonprofit corporations affiliated with religious institutions could exempt themselves from this requirement, for-profit companies had to comply. In a 5–4 decision, the Supreme Court held that it violated the federal Religious Freedom Restoration Act (RFRA) to apply this requirement to closely held for-profit corporations when the religious owners of those corporations had religious objections to the use contraceptives.

The Court said that it had "little trouble concluding" that the contraceptive mandate substantially burdened the corporation's free exercise of religion. The Court said that it would assume that the government has a compelling interest in ensuring the availability of contraceptives for women, but because of the burden on religion the government was required to pursue those interests in a manner that was the "least restrictive" of free exercise concerns. The Court noted that there were less restrictive alternatives. For example, Congress could directly pay for these contraceptives or Congress could allow for-profit companies the same ability to opt out that it had given to not-for-profit companies that are affiliated with religions that oppose contraception. The Court thus concluded that "the contraceptive mandate, as applied to closely held corporations, violates RFRA."[2]

- In *Town of Greece v. Galloway* (2014), the Court held that it did not violate the Establishment Clause for a town board to begin virtually every meeting, as it had for a ten-year period, with a prayer by a Christian minister.[3] The Town of Greece is a suburb of Rochester, New York, of about 100,000 people. Its town board had opened meetings with a moment of silence until 1999 when the town supervisors initiated a policy change. The town began inviting ministers to begin meetings each month with a prayer.

From 1999 to 2007, the town invited exclusively Christian ministers, most of whom gave explicitly Christian prayers. In 2007, complaints were made to the town board about this and for four months clergy from other religions were invited. But then for the next 18 months, the town board reverted to inviting only Christian clergy and their prayers were almost always Christian in their content.

The Court, in a 5–4 decision, held that the Town of Greece did not violate the Establishment Clause. The Court expressed great deference to the government in having prayers before legislative sessions and held: "Absent a pattern of prayers that over time denigrate, proselytize, or betray an impermissible government purpose, a challenge based solely on the content of a prayer will not likely establish a constitutional violation."[4]

- At issue in *Trinity Lutheran Church of Columbia v. Comer* (2017)[5] was a Missouri program that provides funding to qualified schools so that they could resurface their playgrounds. Because of the Missouri Constitution's prohibition against public funding of religious institutions, the state refused to make this aid available to parochial schools. The Supreme Court, in a 7–2 decision, held that Missouri violated the rights of Trinity Lutheran under the Free Exercise Clause of the First Amendment by denying the church an otherwise available public benefit on account of its religious status. Chief Justice Roberts wrote for the Court and said that Missouri was discriminating against religious institutions in the receipt of this benefit. The Court declared: "Trinity Lutheran is a member of the community too, and the State's decision to exclude it for purposes of this public program must withstand the strictest scrutiny."[6] The Court found that Missouri failed to meet strict scrutiny and Chief Justice Roberts concluded his opinion with the powerful statement: "But the exclusion of Trinity Lutheran from a public benefit for which it is otherwise qualified, solely because it is a church, is odious to our Constitution all the same, and cannot stand."[7]

- *Masterpiece Cakeshop, Ltd. v. Colorado Civil Rights Commission* (2018) posed important questions concerning free exercise of religion and freedom of speech but was decided on the ground that government officials had expressed impermissible animus against religion.[8] Charlie Craig and David Mullins got married in Massachusetts and wanted to celebrate their wedding where they lived in Colorado. They went to a local bakery, Masterpiece Cakeshop, a corporation in Colorado, and sought to purchase a wedding cake. The owner, Jack Phillips, refused to design and bake the cake, saying that gay marriage violated his religious beliefs. He said that he would be implicitly complicit in violation of his religion if he were to design and bake the cake. He was willing for his bakery to sell an already prepared cake for the couple but not to make one for them.

  The Colorado Anti-Discrimination Act prohibits businesses from discriminating, including based on sexual orientation. The law provides: "It is a discriminatory practice and unlawful for a person, directly or indirectly, to refuse, withhold from, or deny to an individual or a group, because of disability, race, creed, color, sex, sexual orientation, marital status, national origin, or ancestry, the full and equal enjoyment of the goods, services, facilities, privileges, advantages, or accommodations of a place of public accommodation."[9] Craig and Mullins filed a discrimination complaint against Masterpiece Cakeshop and Phillips in September 2012, shortly after the couple's visit to the shop. The Colorado Civil Rights Commission ruled in favor of Craig and Mullins and the Colorado Court of Appeals affirmed. The Supreme Court reversed in a 7–2 decision. Justice Kennedy wrote for the Court; only Justices Ginsburg and Sotomayor dissented.

The Court did not reach the central issues of the case: Would it violate free exercise of religion or freedom of speech under the First Amendment to force Masterpiece Cakeshop to design and bake a cake for a same-sex wedding? Instead, the Court found that the Colorado Civil Rights Commission had expressed impermissible hostility to religion and thus violated the Free Exercise Clause of the First Amendment. Justice Kennedy wrote: "The Civil Rights Commission's treatment of his case has some elements of a clear and impermissible hostility toward the sincere religious beliefs that motivated his objection."[10]

- In *American Legion v. American Humanist Association*, the Court, in 2019, reversed a lower court and allowed a 32–foot cross on a large pedestal (about 40 feet high altogether) to remain at a busy intersection on public property in Prince George's County, Maryland.[11] In concluding that the large cross did not violate the First Amendment, the Supreme Court stressed that it was put there after World War I as a tribute to those who died in military service and thus should be regarded as a tribute to war dead. Justice Alito, writing for the Court, declared at the outset of his opinion: "The Religion Clauses of the Constitution aim to foster a society in which people of all beliefs can live together harmoniously, and the presence of the Bladensburg Cross on the land where it has stood for so many years is fully consistent with that aim."[12]

- Justice Alito's majority opinion said that the cross "has also taken on a secular meaning. Indeed, there are instances in which its message is now almost entirely secular."[13] The Court stressed that a cross, as in this instance, was a symbol for those who died in a war. Justice Alito wrote: "The Bladensburg Cross carries special significance in commemorating World War I. Due in large part to the image of the simple wooden crosses that originally marked the graves of American soldiers killed in the war, the cross became a symbol of their sacrifice, and the design of the

Bladensburg Cross must be understood in light of that background. That the cross originated as a Christian symbol and retains that meaning in many contexts does not change the fact that the symbol took on an added secular meaning when used in World War I memorials."[14]

- Justice Alito's opinion also emphasized that the cross had been there for a long time and that removing it would be perceived as hostility to religion.

* * *

These are all Supreme Court decisions from the last five years. They involve issues of both the Establishment Clause and the Free Exercise Clause. They reveal the issues that are sure to be litigated in the years ahead. Does *Hobby Lobby* mean that all corporations will be able to invoke religious freedom in seeking an exception from federal laws pursuant to the Religious Freedom Restoration Act? Does *Town of Greece v. Galloway* mean that sectarian religious prayers will be allowed at all government events, except possibly for schools? After *Trinity Lutheran v. Comer* will the Court hold that the government is constitutionally *required* to provide all forms of aid to religious institutions when it gives the assistance to secular private institutions?[15] After *Masterpiece Cakeshop* will businesses be able to discriminate against gays and lesbians—and others—because of the business owners' religious beliefs? After *American Legion v. American Humanist Association* is there any limit on religious symbols on government property?

THE POLITICAL DIVIDE

It is striking that the conservative justices were in the majority in all of these cases and the most liberal justices—Ginsburg and

Sotomayor—were in dissent in every one of them. Some of the decisions were split 5–4 on ideological grounds (such as *Hobby Lobby* and *Town of Greece*), while the rest were 7–2, but always with the conservatives in the majority and the most liberal justices in dissent. This is not coincidence: views on religion and government, and the appropriate content of the First Amendment, are very much defined by political ideology.

There always has been a political dimension to understanding the Constitution's Religion Clauses, but the political landscape has changed in the last few decades. Throughout most of American history, debates about the Constitution and religion occurred in a context where Protestant sects assumed they had a special place in the culture and practices of the country, and where there was a great deal of hostility to religious outliers.[16] Although the framers set the Constitution against notions of established religions and against religious persecution and intolerance, the country did not always live up to these ideals. As we explain in Chapter 2, the framers were very clear about rejecting any sense that Protestants should have a special status in the American republic, but this did not prevent others from integrating Protestant religious practices and imagery into government activity.

In the same way that "all men are created equal" did not prevent whites from infusing white supremacy into American law and culture, the First Amendment did not prevent government invocations of Protestant conceptions of the divine into our government practices and even Protestant notions of prayer into the public schools. The teaching of Darwin in the schools set off a firestorm in the 1920s, and a religion-inspired criminal prosecution of a high school teacher became a media circus.[17] Americans who were not part of the Protestant establishment often found themselves the victims of violence and hatred and were excluded from jobs, schools, and neighborhoods well into the 20th century. In the 19th century anti-Catholic venom was part of the typical school day. In 1834, a convent was burned to the ground by an anti-Catholic mob near Bunker Hill. In Philadelphia in 1844, anti-Catholic sentiment combined with anti-immigrant hostility to fuel the Bible Riots, torching houses, destroying two Catholic churches, and killing 20 people.[18] Mormons were persecuted. Joseph Smith was tarred and feathered by a Protestant mob in 1832 and would later be killed (along with his brother) by a mob in Carthage, Illinois. In 1838 the Missouri governor ordered all Mormons expelled from the state.[19] The Ku Klux Klan brought its campaign of terror to Jews and Catholics as well as African Americans.[20] Jehovah's Witnesses often found themselves harassed and beaten.[21] Native Americans were not even viewed as people with any spiritual life worth respecting.[22]

By the mid-20th century things got better, with religious arrogance, hatred, and intolerance evolving into a more widespread appreciation of religious diversity and inclusion. "The nation that could not forget or forgive the fact that Al Smith was Catholic loved John Fitzgerald Kennedy; and the nation that once tolerated quotas for Jews in its most distinguished medical schools nearly elected Al Gore president on the strength of his energetic running mate, Joseph Liberman."[23] In the wake of the 9/11 (2001) terrorist attacks on the Twin Towers and the Pentagon, President George W. Bush saw fit to visit a mosque to stand in solidarity with Islamic Americans. Muslim women have now been elected to the Congress.

Contemporary debates take place in the wake of the collapse of the presumptive Protestant establishment and with much diminished animus toward people of different faith traditions. Very few judges and scholars defend the view that Protestant practices and assumptions should be a formal part of government activity, meaning that there is more separation between church and state than was the case throughout most of our history. There are also fewer efforts by government officials to use the law as a weapon against disfavored religious practitioners, or against people such as John Scopes who stood up to religious majorities.

Nevertheless, the country is still deeply divided on questions relating to the proper understanding of the Religion Clauses. As the recent cases demonstrate, most of these divides are over whether mainstream religious activity should still be supported by government or accommodated through the granting of exemptions from ordinary social duties, in cases where the law no longer reflects conservative Protestant beliefs about proper social policy. Indeed, these claims might be seen as the Protestant establishment fighting back against their loss of privilege, just as in other parts of American politics we see whites fighting back against challenges to their historically dominant position in American culture, society, and government.[24]

This explanation, though, does not account for the shift in the political landscape with regard to religion. As recently as the 1940s, Southern Baptists and Orthodox Jews strongly favored the separation of church and state. Perhaps because they were fearful of government regulation of religion and maybe because they could not imagine the government helping their faiths, they espoused the view that the Establishment Clause prevented government aid to religion and religion's involvement with government.

This began to change, though, with the 1964 election. The Barry Goldwater campaign for president engaged Southern Christian evangelicals who opposed desegregation.[25] Some who had been part of the Goldwater campaign became architects for a new Republican Party, one founded less on anti-communist appeals. They called themselves "The New Right."

Paul Weyrich, who had been a volunteer for Goldwater in 1964, founded the Heritage Foundation in 1973—a think tank to promote the ideas of the New Right.[26] Weyrich also founded ALEC, the American Legislative Exchange Council, in 1973 to coordinate the work of Religious Right state legislators. It was funded primarily by large corporations, industry groups, and conservative foundations—including R. J. Reynolds, Koch Industries, and the American Petroleum Institute. In 1979, Weyrich coined the term "Moral Majority." The goal was to politicize members of fundamentalist, Pentecostal, and charismatic churches—a constituency that had been basically apolitical. Paul Weyrich, speaking in Dallas in 1980, captured the spirit of this new movement. He said, "We are talking about Christianizing America. We are talking about simply spreading the gospel in a political context."[27] Jerry Falwell, who became the leader of the Moral Majority, said, "Get them saved, get them Baptized, and get them registered."[28]

The 1980 presidential election saw the emergence of the religious right as a major political force. Thousands of fundamentalist preachers participated in political training seminars that year, and by June, the religious right registered more than two million voters as Republicans.[29] Their goal was to register five million new voters by November.[30] In the 1980 elections, the newly politicized Religious Right succeeded in unseating five of the most liberal Democrat incumbents in the US Senate and provided the margin that helped Ronald Reagan defeat Jimmy Carter. Many other organizations formed in the 1980s to harness religion as a political force; all were conservative.

The Reverend Timothy La Haye founded the American Coalition for Traditional Values—a network of 110,000 churches—committed to getting Christian candidates elected to office.[31] In 1979, Beverly and Tim LaHaye founded Concerned Women for America (CWA) claiming a membership of 600,000. With prayer and action meetings, the women were, and still are, a formidable lobbying force.

The result of this has been to link conservative Republican politics to the religious right. President Nixon was the first president to institute weekly White House chapel services.[32] According to historian Garry Wills, the institution of prayer breakfasts was an attempt by the Nixon White House to woo the rising evangelical community.[33] Nixon proposed substantial increases in government funding for parochial schools, including tax credits for parents who were paying tuition for religious education for their children.

Nixon, though, was mild in his opposition to the separation of church and state compared with Ronald Reagan. President Reagan was a frequent critic of the idea of such a wall. President Reagan said that in drafting the First Amendment our Founding Fathers "sought to protect churches from government interference" but "never intended to construct a wall of hostility between government and the concept of religious belief itself."[34] President Reagan urged the "reawaken[ing] of America's religious and moral heart, recognizing that a deep and abiding faith in God is the rock upon which this great nation is founded."[35]

President Reagan repeatedly criticized the Supreme Court's decisions banning prayer in public schools and said that "well meaning Americans in the name of freedom have taken freedom away. For the sake of religious tolerance they've forbidden religious practice in our classrooms."[36] On May 17, 1982, President Reagan proposed an amendment to the United States Constitution to allow prayer in public schools. It read: "Nothing in this Constitution shall be construed to prohibit individual or group prayer in public schools or other public institutions. No person shall be required by the United States or any state to participate in prayer."[37] In presenting the amendment to Congress, he described school prayer as a "simple freedom" and a "fundamental part of our American heritage." In his 1983 State of the Union Address, President Reagan declared that "God should never have been expelled from America's classrooms in the first place."[38]

In 2004, when George W. Bush won a close reelection bid over challenger John Kerry, one out of four Republican voters self-identified as an evangelical Christian. Religions, such as Southern

Baptists, that as recently as the 1940s urged a separation of church and state, shifted to opposing any such notions. The religious right forcefully argued that the insistence on a secular government was impermissible hostility to religion. Donald Trump has vigorously courted support from conservative Christians and has won praise from them for fulfilling " 'wish lists' of steps they hoped he'd take to oppose abortion and rein in the LGBTQ-rights movement."[39]

Not surprisingly, this shift in the political landscape is reflected in the ideology of justices on the Supreme Court. Conservatives, politically and in the judiciary, want to accommodate religion. Liberals want to separate government and religion. Our central focus in this book is what it will mean that there is now—and will be for the foreseeable future—a Court with five conservative justices who are very likely to take the conservative position on the First Amendment's Religion Clauses.

The ideas of "accommodation" and "separation" are useful for both the Establishment Clause and the Free Exercise Clause. The "separation" view of the Establishment Clause is that it is meant—in the words of Thomas Jefferson—to create a wall that separates church and state.[40] Under this view, to the greatest extent realistic, the government should be secular and the place for religion is in the private realm of people's homes, places of worship, and daily lives. This view would very much limit the presence of religion in government activities (such as through prayer or religious symbols) and government support for religious institutions.

The "accommodation" view of the Establishment Clause says that the provision should be interpreted to accommodate religion in government and government support for religion. It flatly rejects that there should be a wall separating church and state. This approach to the Establishment Clause provides that the government violates this provision only if it coerces religious participation or discriminates among religions in the awarding of government benefits. For example, Justice Scalia wrote that "the coercion that was a hallmark of historical establishments of religion was coercion of religious orthodoxy and of financial support *by force of law and threat of penalty*."[41] Justice Kennedy said that "the Establishment Clause ... guarantees at a minimum that a government may not coerce anyone to support or participate in religion or its exercise, or otherwise act in a way which establishes a [state] religion or religious faith, or tends to do so."[42] The accommodationist view believes that religion can be a part of government activities, such as with prayer or with religious symbols, so long as there is no coercion. The accommodationist view is untroubled by government aid to religious institutions, and indeed believes that it violates free exercise of religion to deny benefits to religious institutions that are provided to secular private institutions.

As for the Free Exercise Clause, the "separation" view is that government should stay out of the business of worship and the internal operations of religious institutions; that is, it requires that the government not act with animus toward religion. But this approach does not otherwise offer religious people special accommodations when the government is merely passing neutral laws of general applicability. Instead it expects all people to live by the same rules when the government is acting in its secular capacity. It stresses that people cannot inflict injury on others, such as discriminating against them, based on religious freedom.

This approach is reflected in the Court's 1990 decision in *Employment Division v. Smith*.[43] *Smith* involved a challenge by Native Americans to an Oregon law prohibiting use of peyote, a hallucinogenic substance. Specifically, individuals challenged the state's determination that their religious use of peyote, which resulted in their dismissal from employment, was misconduct disqualifying them from receipt of unemployment compensation benefits.

Justice Scalia, writing for the majority, rejected the claim that free exercise of religion required an exemption from an otherwise valid law. He said that "we have never held that an individual's religious beliefs excuse him from compliance with an otherwise valid law prohibiting conduct that the State is free to regulate."[44] Scalia thus declared "that the right of free exercise does not relieve an individual of the obligation to comply with a 'valid and neutral law of general applicability on the ground that the law proscribes (or prescribes) conduct that his religion prescribes (or proscribes).'"[45] To rule otherwise would force courts to "determine the 'centrality' of religious beliefs before applying a 'compelling interest' test in the free exercise field," leading Scalia to ask, "What principle of law or logic can be brought to bear to contradict a believer's assertion that a particular act is 'central' to his personal faith?"[46] This sentiment echoed Justice Stevens's earlier objections to offering special accommodations to religious practitioners, where he emphasized "the overriding interest in keeping the government—whether the legislature or the courts—out of the business of evaluating the relative merits of differing religious claims," because to do otherwise would run the risk that "governmental approval of some and disapproval of others will be perceived as favoring one religion over another" in violation of the Establishment Clause.[47] Simply put, separation means that government should not be entangled in religious matters.

The "accommodation" view of the Free Exercise Clause is that strict scrutiny is required when the government substantially burdens religion, and that whenever possible the government must adopt the approach that imposes the least restriction on religious liberty, even if that means exempting religious practitioners from laws that everyone else has to obey. This was the approach prescribed in *Sherbert v. Verner* in 1963,[48] and it was the approach that Congress insisted on when it passed the Religious Freedom Restoration Act and the Religious Land Use and Institutionalized Persons Act. It is the approach that was the focus in *Burwell v. Hobby Lobby*.

So, for example, in *Masterpiece Cakeshop*, the owner of the bakery, Jack Phillips, urged that the Court accommodate his religious beliefs by holding that liability under the Colorado civil rights law would violate his free exercise of religion. But the plaintiffs, Charlie Craig and David Mullins, argued that the First Amendment does not require such accommodation and that no exception should be created to the Colorado civil rights law based on religion.[49]

COMPETING APPROACHES

At the risk of oversimplifying, we can identify four possible positions with regard to the Establishment Clause and the Free Exercise Clause, with these "clusters" of approaches reflecting views that have been adopted by judges and scholars at various times:

- *Separation Establishment Clause/Separation Free Exercise Clause*
- *Accommodation Establishment Clause/Accommodation Free Exercise Clause*
- *Separation Establishment Clause/Accommodation Free Exercise Clause*
- *Accommodation Establishment Clause/Separation Free Exercise Clause*

This presentation of the four positions is an over-simplification because for both the Establishment Clause and the Free Exercise Clause there are continuums. On the Establishment Clause, for example, the most accommodating version is Justice Thomas's view that the provision does not apply to state and local governments at all and as to the federal government, it applies only to legislative activity.[50] For those who take the view that coercion is required, there is the question whether mere social pressure is sufficient or whether only legal requirements under penalty of law can violate the Constitution.[51] Justice O'Connor articulated a middle view on the Establishment Clause that the government acts unconstitutionally only if it endorses religion or a specific religion. She wrote that "every government practice must be judged in its unique circumstances to determine whether it constitutes an endorsement or disapproval of religion."[52]

In the 1960s and 1970s, the Supreme Court followed the separation approach to the Establishment Clause but the accommodation approach to the Free Exercise Clause. That is, Court majorities adopted the view that the Establishment Clause requires *separation* of church and state, but the Free Exercise Clause required *accommodation* for religious practitioners and that the burdening of religion had to meet strict scrutiny analysis. In 1990, in *Employment Division v. Smith*, the Court shifted to a separation approach to the Free Exercise Clause. The recent decisions on the Establishment Clause—such as *Town of Greece v. Galloway* and *American Legion v. American Humanist Association*—reflect the Court adopting an accommodationist view of the Establishment Clause.

The correspondence between ideology and these views has not been constant. In the 1940s, many religions, including fundamentalist ones, strongly favored separation of church and state. In recent decades, these same religions have favored an accommodationist view of the Establishment Clause. There would be no disagreement that today conservatives endorse the accommodationist view of the Establishment Clause, while liberals favor a separationist approach. That is why the conservatives were in the majority in cases like *Town of Greece v. Galloway* and *American Legion v. American Humanist Association*, while the most liberal justices, Ginsburg and Sotomayor, dissented.

For free exercise, it is more complicated. *Employment Division v. Smith*, which embodies the separationist view of the Free Exercise Clause, was written by Justice Scalia. Scalia also adopted an accommodationist view of the Establishment Clause (thus reversing the approaches to each that were dominant in the 1960s and early '70s). *Smith* involved whether free exercise of religion was violated when a Native American church was denied an exception to a state's peyote law when it wanted to use the substance in traditional religious rites. One can wonder whether Justice Scalia, who wrote the opinion, and the majority would have come out the same way if it was Christians or Jews being denied the sacramental use of wine.

In more recent years, the conservatives have come to prefer a much stronger protection of free exercise of religion, such as to allow businesses to deny contraceptive coverage to their employees (*Burwell v. Hobby Lobby*) and to discriminate against gays and lesbians (*Masterpiece Cakeshop v. Colorado Civil Rights Commission*). Certainly, *Trinity Lutheran* suggests a much more robust Free Exercise Clause, with the conservatives indicating that the government is required to provide at least some benefits to religious institutions when they are given to private secular institutions.

In fact, there now well may be a majority on the Court willing to overrule *Employment Division v. Smith* and provide more constitutional protection for free exercise claims. In 2019, in *Kennedy v. Bremerton School District*, the Supreme Court refused to hear the appeal of a football coach who had been fired for kneeling and praying on the field. The lower courts ruled against the coach's claim that his firing violated his freedom of speech. Justice Alito wrote an opinion, joined by Justices Thomas, Gorsuch, and Kavanaugh, in which he said that the coach still had live claims, not presented in the petition for certiorari, under the Free Exercise Clause and under Title VII, for employment discrimination based on religion.[53]

Justice Alito concluded his opinion: "In *Employment Div., Dept. of Human Resources of Ore. v. Smith* (1990), the Court drastically cut back on the protection provided by the Free Exercise Clause, and in *Trans World Airlines, Inc. v. Hardison* (1977), the Court opined that Title VII's prohibition of discrimination on the basis of religion does not require an employer to make any accommodation that imposes more than a *de minimis* burden. In this case, however, we have not been asked to revisit those decisions."[54] It well may be that these four justices—and perhaps Chief Justice Roberts—want to reconsider and overrule *Employment Division v. Smith*. In fact, the Supreme Court has granted review in a case to be argued in October 2020, *Fulton v. City of Philadelphia, Pennsylvania* on the question of whether "whether *Employment Division v. Smith* should be revisited."

Our prediction is that we are in an accommodationist era for the Establishment Clause, as there are likely five justices to adopt the view that the government only violates this provision of the First Amendment if it coerces religious participation or discriminates among religions in awarding benefits. At the same time, we also are seeing the emergence of an accommodationist approach to the Free Exercise Clause, where there are five justices to protect the ability of businesses and others to discriminate and deny benefits based on their religious views.

OUR THESIS

In this book, we seek to be both descriptive and normative. We wish to describe the law of the Establishment Clause and the Free Exercise Clause, and how it has developed, as carefully and as accurately as we can. But at the same time, we express our views of the proper approach to these constitutional provisions. Our thesis is that the Constitution meant to and should be interpreted as creating a secular republic, meaning that the government has no role in advancing religion and that religious belief and practice should be a private matter, one where people should not be able to inflict injury on others in the name of religion. In other words, in this book, we detail and defend the separationist view for both the Establishment Clause and the Free Exercise Clause, and we warn against the emerging accommodationist approach to each of these clauses.

For the Establishment Clause, we defend the view that the First Amendment was meant to create a wall that separates church and state. Under our approach, prayer should not be part of government activities, religious symbols do not belong on government property, and the government should be very limited in its ability to give aid directly to religious institutions.

Likewise, for the Free Exercise Clause, we take a separationist view. Our approach protects religious beliefs and the internal operation of religions from government interference. But it does not provide a basis for a religious exemption from a neutral secular law. Thus, we believe that *Hobby Lobby* and *Masterpiece Cakeshop* were wrongly decided: the government can make sure that women have access to contraceptives and that anti-discrimination laws are enforced. We disagree with the Court's holding in *Trinity Lutheran* that the government is constitutionally required to provide aid to religious institutions when it provides such aid to secular private institutions.

The book has a simple organization. Chapter 2 provides a history of the origins of the Religion Clauses and sets the stage for our claim that a separationist approach is justified if we properly understand the concerns of the framers. Chapter 3 looks in more detail at the main approaches judges and scholars have adopted toward the Establishment Clause and elaborates our argument for why a separationist approach is best. Chapter 4 does the same with respect to the Free Exercise Clause, criticizing the accommodation approach and defending the separation view. Finally, in Chapter 5 we conclude by addressing the criticism that our approach is anti-religion while the accommodationist approach should be regarded as pro-religion, and we explain why separation does not mean hostility toward religion.

Our focus is on these two provisions of the First Amendment. Thus, we do not discuss state constitutional law except in passing. Nor do we focus much on federal and state statutes dealing with religion.

We write at a time of enormous political divisiveness. There is no doubt that there is great ideological division on issues regarding religion and government, both on the Supreme Court and in society. This book is our effort to describe that division and express our views about how the Religion Clauses of the First Amendment should be interpreted and understood.

CHAPTER TWO

The Concerns of the Founders

IN THE CENTURY and a half leading up to America's Declaration of Independence, England was consumed by violent, destabilizing, and oppressive battles over the relationship between government and religion. An inter-faith marriage triggered a political crisis that led to the dissolution of Parliament. Rebellions broke out over religious divisions. Religious intrigue led one king to negotiate an invasion of his country on condition that certain religious sects be declared an established religion of the realm. There were ongoing and costly persecutions of so-called non-conformists and dissenters from the official Church of England, leading tens of thousands of Puritans, Anabaptists, Lutherans, and others to flee England to mainland Europe and North America. Others stayed to lead a revolutionary struggle against the English Crown. In the resulting civil wars, a higher percentage of the English population was killed than were killed during the First World War. Kings lost their heads or fled their kingdoms.[1]

During this period, debates intensified over the wisdom and propriety of having government aligned with what it considered to be the one true religion. The prevailing instinct was to double-down on this long-established tradition—for example, by declaring that all religious practices had to conform to a government-created prayer book and forbidding anyone from holding a government office who held a deviant religious view. But some reformers, including John Milton and John Locke, were inspired by the chaos and destruction to pen arguments advocating a new "tolerance" on the part of government for diversity of religious thought and practice.[2]

Over the next century these battles and debates transformed age-old ideas about the source of political authority and the conditions necessary for political stability. In 1600, few Englishmen doubted that government and church should cooperate to maintain and spread the one true religion. By 1800, Americans had formally embraced toleration of religious diversity and were on a path to shed the practice of formally linking government to particular religious establishments.

Those who framed the American Constitution insisted that the welfare of the people was best advanced, not by religious *establishments* and forced *conformity* to officially endorsed religions, but by the *secularization* of government authority and the *toleration* of diverse religious practitioners. Unlike the French revolutionaries, who formally rejected religion as a worthwhile feature of civic life and launched a campaign to "dechristianize" France,[3] the American Founders stayed true to the concerns of the early colonists regarding the importance of religious freedom. But unlike the original colonists, the Founders—having benefited from greater historical experience and exposure to newer arguments by reformers—concluded that it was vital to separate governing authority from religious authority.

By the time the American Republic was founded there would be no references in the founding documents to a Supreme Being, no authority given to Congress to legislate on matters of religion, and a prohibition against religious tests for office. At the state level there were vestiges of formal, government authorized "established" religions, but state practices were quickly changing. An establishment of religion (in terms of direct tax aid for a favored church) was the practice in nine of the thirteen British colonies on the eve of the American Revolution, but by 1800 only three American states (New Hampshire, Massachusetts, and Connecticut) had established churches.[4] Some of the arguments associated with this transformation—especially during Virginia's multi-year debate about assessments in support of particular churches—became among the most important and revered documents in all of American history.

In this chapter we trace the major events and debates that shaped the drafting of the Constitution and the First Amendment's Religion Clauses. We do not support an "originalist" approach to constitutional interpretation, which believes that the meaning of a constitutional provision is determined by its original understanding. But we do believe that contemporary debates should be informed by the concerns of the framers, who understood the dangers of religious establishments and the threats to religious liberty and thought it important to avoid the bloody and oppressive mistakes of their forefathers. We, of course, recognize that there was not unanimity at the founding as to the appropriate relationship between government and religion. That said, we think that there was a consensus among the majority of those who drafted and ratified the Constitution and the Religion Clauses in the First Amendment that there should be a secular government with protection of individual religious freedom.

DEBATES DURING THE PRE-COLONIAL AND COLONIAL ERAS

In 17th-century England it was natural for government to appoint religious ministers, pay their salaries, sponsor religious ceremonies, and require all subjects to worship God in a particular way. The Act of Uniformity set out the principles and practices that established the Anglican Church in Great Britain and declared that all religious practice had to conform to a legislatively mandated prayer book. The Test Act of 1673 detailed the penalties and disabilities imposed upon those who dissented from the Church of England.[5] When King James II attempted to suspend the act in order to accommodate Catholics, he set in motion a chain of events that forced him to flee his realm.

Those religious dissenters who fled England for North America brought with them a desire to practice their religion but no initial impulse to accommodate religious dissenters who might be among them. The colonists did not follow the lead of Dutch Protestants, who ensured that minority religions were protected after the Netherlands gained independence. Instead, the American colonists followed the lead of Spanish and Portuguese Catholic colonizers who ventured to Latin America, the Caribbean, Mexico, and modern-day Florida, where they sought to establish governments that were aligned with the one true church as they understood it.[6]

The first colonial charters established Protestant Christian commonwealths, with some differences in favored churches. Virginia, for example, favored the Church of England, while Massachusetts was dominated by Puritans/Congregationalists. But whatever the favored religion, the resulting union of church and state comprised both establishment (e.g., colonies built churches, paid ministers, organized religious activity) and conformity. Conformity was accomplished through a combination of legal compulsion to attend specific religious services and the imposition of burdens on members of disfavored religions, for example, by denying them political rights.[7]

Nevertheless, the multiplicity of sects in the colonies, combined with ongoing immigration and the desire to attract higher numbers of settlers, created a context for new arguments about the wisdom of tolerating diverse religious views and practices. Religious battles in England were focused on aligning all of England with the one true faith. By contrast, within the North American colonies there was a plurality of practices; no one pursued the project of aligning all of the colonies with the one true faith. As a result, individuals who experienced life as part of a colonial religious majority in one place might find themselves objects of oppression if they traveled elsewhere. Anglicans who had been content in Virginia might realize, after moving to Connecticut and Massachusetts, that they were required to pay taxes to support Congregationalist churches.[8]

There were some early examples of European dissenters embracing experiments in religious liberty. William Penn advertised in Germany for non-Quaker settlers by promising them religious freedom if they came. Later, based on his experiences with religious toleration, he advised King Charles II that "Peace, Plenty, and Safety, the three great Inducements to any Country to Honour the Prince, and Love the Government, as well as the best Allurements to Foreigners to trade with it and transport themselves to it, are utterly lost by such Partialities" involving restrictions on religious liberty. Maryland was founded by Catholic leader Lord Baltimore as an experiment in Catholic and Protestant coexistence. The Maryland Toleration Act (1649) declared that government could not "molest" any form of private Christian worship (but also sentenced to death anyone who denied the divinity of Jesus).[9]

However, this experiment in tolerance was short-lived. The act was revoked five years later, and by 1702 the Church of England was formally established as Maryland's official religion, with Catholics disenfranchised in 1718.[10]

A more lasting legacy was created by Roger Williams, considered the founder of religious freedom in the United States. He sided with the Puritans who insisted on a complete separation with the Anglican Church. But rather than replace the Anglican Church with a more purified church, Williams advocated for the complete separation of church and state. Exiled from Massachusetts in 1635, he settled in what is now Providence, Rhode Island, and founded the Rhode Island Colony, which declared in its charter, "No person within the said colony, at any time hereafter, shall be any ways molested, punished, disquieted, or called in question, for any differences in opinion in matters of religion, and do not actually disturb the peace of our said colony; but that all and every person and persons may, from time to time, and at all times hereafter, freely and fully have and enjoy his and their own judgments and consciences, in matters of religious concernments." His goal, as he famously put it in 1643, was to construct "a wall of separation between the garden of the Church and the wilderness of the world."[11]

Williams's work, *The Bloudy Tenent of Persecution, for Cause of Conscience, Discussed in a Conference between Truth and Peace*, was published in England in 1644—the same year John Milton published *Areopagitica* to make the case for more liberty of expression (especially for Protestant non-conformists)—while he was trying to convince English authorities to grant Rhode Island a charter. The book was so radical that Parliament ordered every copy burned. But it had a substantial influence throughout the colonies. In it Milton lamented "the blood of so many hundred thousand souls of *Protestants* and *Papists*, split in the *Wars* of *present* and *former Ages*, for their respective *Consciences*"—noting that the spilling of this blood "is not *required* nor *accepted* by *Jesus Christ* the *Prince of Peace*"—and argued that the "*enforced uniformity*" of religion in any "*civil state* . . . is the greatest occasion of *civil War, ravishing of conscience, persecution of Christ Jesus* in his servants, and of the *hypocrisy* and *destruction* of *millions of souls*." In the middle of this bloody century, and at the dawn of the English Civil War, Williams's advice was that a "firm and lasting *peace*" could only be procured by the "permission of other *consciences* and *worships* than a state professes."[12]

In the decades that followed, England continued to experience conflict arising from futile efforts to impose religious conformity on a society that had experienced a rapid multiplication of churches and sects, and eventually leaders began to see the wisdom of Williams's advice, at least as regards toleration for Protestant non-conformists.[13] John Locke's A *Letter Concerning Toleration*, written in 1685 and published in 1689 (a year after the Glorious Revolution), reflected on all the civil unrest in order to argue for greater separation between the concerns of the state and the concerns of the church. In separating church and state he distinguished "civil society," which involves itself with "life, liberty, healthy, and indolence of the body; and the possession of outward things, such as money, lands, houses, furniture, and the like," with matters of the soul:

> The care of souls is not committed to the civil magistrate . . . because it appears not that God has ever given any such authority to one man over another as to compel anyone to his religion . . . [since] all the life and power of true religion consists in the inward and full persuasion of the mind; and faith is not faith without believing. . . . If a Roman Catholic believe that to be really the body of Christ which another man calls bread, he does no injury thereby to his neighbor. If a Jew do not believe the New Testament to be the Word of God, he does not thereby alter anything in men's civil rights. . . . The power of the magistrate and the estates of the people may be equally secure whether any man believe these things or no.[14]

Locke's *Letter* provided a philosophical elaboration of the thinking behind the Toleration Act of 1689, part of an effort to assure a constitutional settlement of the Glorious Revolution of 1688, with a focus on getting Protestants who were not members of the Church of England to support the settlement. (The Dutch Protestant, William of Orange, who was now on the throne, had experienced religious pluralism in the Netherlands.) The act secured freedom of worship to Protestant non-conformists who had pledged oaths of Allegiance and Supremacy and rejected transubstantiation. It also set a new standard for religious dissent in the American colonies, with Baptists, Methodists, and Quakers using the document to request exemptions from taxes that were used to support established churches.[15]

These were the initial steps that would eventually lead to the privatization of religious practice, whereby civil society forgoes the impulse to impose a religious orthodoxy on a community, and where people with different beliefs would be left alone so long as they did not interfere with the imperatives of secular government. By 1744 it was possible even for a Puritan preacher, Elisha Williams, who also happened to be the rector of Yale University, to write, "Every man has an equal right to follow the dictates of his own conscience in the affairs of religion" and "to follow his judgment wherever it leads him; even an equal right with any rulers be they civil or ecclesiastical."[16]

There were still lingering concerns that certain religious faiths and practices might be inconsistent even with a more tolerant government. The Toleration Act excluded from its protections Catholics, non-trinitarians, and atheists. In the colonies, even when there was an impulse to allow individuals freedom of conscience, there were still debates about the limits of tolerance.

The most important political controversy testing religious tolerance was over whether Quakers and other religious pacifists should be required to perform military service. These conflicts were particularly intense in Pennsylvania, where Quaker leader William Penn had instituted an experiment in religious liberty, declaring that no person who acknowledged God and professed to live peaceably could be "molested or prejudiced for their religious persuasion, or practice, in matters of faith and worship." Benjamin Franklin's view was that a policy of voluntary compliance with the militia service was the only policy that satisfied the needs of the community and the rights of conscience. On the eve of the Revolution, pamphleteers insisted that Quakers should receive no special treatment from the general obligation to be available for the militia, arguing, "We know of no Distinctions of Sects, when we meet our Fellow Citizens on Matters of Public Concern, and ask those conscientiously scrupulous against bearing Arms, to contribute toward the Experience of our Opposition, no because of their *religious Persuasion*, but because the general Defense of the Province demands it." More generally, colonial religious dissenters did not seek a right to be exempted from civil law whenever it conflicted with their perceived higher objections, but instead sought the repeal of those laws that required the maintenance of religious establishments, such as taxation to support a church. Other than debates about the military obligations of pacifists, arguments about religious freedom were mostly associated with advocacy for disestablishment rather than advocacy for special exemptions for religious practitioners from the obligation to obey general laws.[17]

A century after the Glorious Revolution, the American colonies provided far less support for religion and mandated far less religious observance than had been the case during the original establishment of the colonies. But these were only first steps. On the eve of the American Revolution most colonial English subjects considered themselves living in a Christian commonwealth. The major legal treatise of this era, William Blackstone's *Commentaries on the Laws of England* (1773), still detailed the many offenses against religion that the government could and should punish. "Christianity," he proclaimed, "is a part of the laws of England."[18] Still, it would be more than ten years before the Constitution would be ratified, and the founding generation had not yet finished debating the relationship between church and state.

THE DEBATES LEADING UP TO THE DRAFTING OF THE
RELIGION CLAUSES

The Revolutionary War ushered in revolutionary thinking about the nature of church-state relations. Of the nine colonies that had established religions, five disestablished immediately—three in the South (North Carolina, South Carolina, and Georgia), and two in the North (New York and Maryland), all places where Anglicanism had dominated.[19]

The idea that individuals had rights of conscience also worked its way into most of the state constitutions created in the wake of the Declaration of Independence. Of the ten state constitutions that mentioned religion, all guaranteed "liberty of conscience." While some limited the liberty to Protestants, there was a growing consensus regarding the rights that should be extended to Catholics, Jews, "Mohammadeans," and other non-Christians.[20] Of the nineteen state constitutions written between 1776 and 1800, every one included a protection for religious freedom, and most also included a provision such as Georgia's (1798) stating, "Nor shall any person be denied the enjoyment of any civil right merely on account of his religious principles." New York's Constitution of 1777 guaranteed religious freedom without discrimination or preference, "*Provided*, That the liberty of conscience, hereby granted, shall not be so construed as to excuse acts of licentiousness, or to justify practices inconsistent with the peace or safety of this state." The 1780 Massachusetts Constitution, drafted primarily by John Adams, included a provision declaring that "no subject shall be hurt, molested, or restrained, in his person, liberty, or estate, for worshipping God in the manner and season most agreeable to the dictates of his own conscience, or for his religious profession of sentiments; provided he doth not disturb the peace or obstruct others in their religious worship." Of the five states that wrote more than one constitution during this period, four increased religious freedom, with the fifth (Pennsylvania) already having strong protections. Although there were some questions and debates about exempting religious practitioners from the force of intrusive laws, most state constitutions assumed that religions did not grant religious practitioners exemptions from the obligations imposed on everyone else by civil law.[21]

During this period, debates about state-established or supported religions were more controversial, although popular support for this practice was weakening. At the time of the Declaration of Independence, Virginia had established a range of practices in support of Anglicanism, but they were quickly being erased. The legislature repealed laws making it a crime to subvert Anglicanism and failing to attend church. In the 1780s James Madison and Thomas Jefferson—no fans of the "age of Constantine" that resulted in "millions of innocent men, women, and children [being] burnt, tortured, fined, and imprisoned" with no resulting consensus on matters of faith[22]—engaged in a lengthy campaign for religious freedom in Virginia. Their campaign ended with the passage of the Virginia Act for Religious Freedom, the law that disestablished the Anglican Church.

The controversy in Virginia began in 1784 when Patrick Henry proposed that a property tax be levied on all citizens to support ministers of recognized Christian sects, with each property owner to specify the denomination to which he wished his tax directed. An amendment was initially passed to drop the word "Christian" so that the act would support all religious instruction, but Benjamin Harrison, the former governor, had the change reversed. The purpose of the bill was to keep the Christian ministry, particularly the Episcopalian clergy, active and solvent.[23]

The next year Madison drafted the "Memorial and Remonstrance against Religious Assessments" arguing that the religion "of every man must be left to the conviction and conscience of every man" and therefore "it is the duty of every man to render to the Creator such homage and such only as he believes to be acceptable to him." He went on:

> Whilst we assert for ourselves a freedom to embrace, to profess and to observe the Religion which we believe to be of divine origin, we cannot deny an equal freedom to those whose minds have not yet yielded to the evidence which has convinced us. If this freedom be abused, it is an offence against God, not against man.

In critiquing the proposed law, Madison echoed Locke's argument in *A Letter Concerning Toleration* advocating a separation of civil authority and religious authority:

> The Bill implies either that the Civil Magistrate is a competent Judge of Religious Truth; or that he may employ Religion as an engine of civil policy. The first is an arrogant pretension falsified by the contradictory opinions of Rulers in all ages, and throughout the world: the second an unhallowed perversion of the means of salvation. . . . [The Bill] will destroy that moderation and harmony which the forbearance of our laws to intermeddle with Religion has produced among its several sects. Torrents of blood have been spilt in the old world, by vain attempts of the secular arm, to extinguish Religious discord, by proscribing all difference in Religious opinion. Time has at length revealed the true remedy. Every relaxation of narrow and rigorous policy, wherever it has been tried, has been found to assuage the disease.[24]

Importantly, Madison was not merely urging a principle of "equality" or "no favoritism" among Protestant sects. Rather, he is urging a more general principle of "noncognizance," meaning that the civil authority can take no notice of such matters and should assert no jurisdiction over a person's faith and conscience. As such, his views presage arguments during debates about the First Amendment regarding laws that "respect an Establishment of religion."[25]

Virginia politicians waited until the 1786 state election before finalizing a decision on these debates. The election brought a strong anti-assessment contingent into the legislature, and the resulting "Act for Establishing Religious Freedom" (1786), drafted by Jefferson, disestablished the Anglican Church in Virginia. In so doing the act declared

> that the impious presumption of legislators and rulers . . . who, being themselves but fallible and uninspired men have assumed dominion over the faith of others, setting up their own opinions and modes of thinking as the only true and infallible, and as such endeavoring to impose them on others, hath established and maintained false religions over the greatest part of world and through all time; that to compel a man to furnish contributions of money for the propagation of opinions which he disbelieves is sinful and tyrannical; . . . that our civil rights have no dependence on our religious opinions any more than our opinions in physics or geometry . . . and finally that Truth is great, and will prevail if left to herself, that she is the proper and sufficient antagonist to error, and has nothing to fear from the conflict, unless by human interposition disarmed of her natural weapons free argument and debate, errors ceasing to be dangerous when it is permitted freely to contradict them.[26]

The bill was one of the three accomplishments Jefferson insisted be mentioned on his tombstone, along with authoring the Declaration of Independence and founding the University of Virginia.

By 1791, the fiery Baptist preacher John Leland was denouncing all establishments of religion, pointing out that when "uninspired, fallible men make their own opinions tests of orthodoxy" then "persecution rages" and religion is stunted by the view that it is "nothing but a trick of state."[27] Acknowledging the different and evolving practices in the states, the Establishment Clause of the First Amendment was designed primarily to prohibit the Congress from interfering in state decisions on this issue.[28] Eleven of the thirteen states had some form of establishment when the Constitution was ratified, and the Establishment Clause ensured that Congress could do nothing to prevent Massachusetts from establishing the Congregational Church, Virginia from establishing the Anglican Church, and Pennsylvania from having no established church.[29]

Still, if states were going to be left free to have different approaches, this meant that the federal government could have no favorites. At the time of the founding, some states had Christian religious tests for legislators, but Article VI of the US Constitution asserts, "No religious Test shall ever be required as a Qualification to any Office of public Trust under the United States." As explained by Oliver Ellsworth (a member of the Constitutional Convention and future Supreme Court justice), "The sole purpose and effect [of this provision] is to exclude persecution, and to secure to you the important right of religious liberty. We are almost the only people in the world, who have a full enjoyment of this important right of human nature. In our country every man has a right to worship God in that way which is most agreeable to his own conscience." Importantly, then, even before the passage of the First Amendment, Article VI of the Constitution incorporated a separation of church and state. As explained by Joseph Story in his *Commentaries on the Constitution*,

[this clause] cut off forever every pretense of any alliance between church and state in the national government. The framers
of the constitution were fully sensible of the dangers from this
course . . . [knowing] that intolerance was ever ready to arm itself
with all the terrors of the civil power to exterminate those, who
doubted its dogmas, or resisted its infallibility.[30]

The provision entered the Constitution with ease during the
drafting but created some drama in the ratifying conventions,
where some expressed a lingering belief that religious or Christian
credentials were a prerequisite for leadership in the Republic. In
the Massachusetts ratifying convention, Colonel Jones of Bristol
expressed the view that "the rulers ought to believe in God or
Christ" and "if our public men were to be of those who had a good
standing in the church, it would be happy for the United States." At
the North Carolina convention, William Lancaster noted that "in
reviewing the qualifications necessary for a President, I did not suppose that the pope could occupy the President's chair. But let us
remember that we form a government for millions not yet in existence. . . . In the course of four or five hundred years, I do not know
how it will work. This is most certain, that Papists may occupy that
chair, and Mahometans make take it. I see nothing against it. There
is a disqualification, I believe, in every state in the Union—it ought
to be so in this system."[31]

There is no doubt that there were those during the founding
period who believed that the new government of the United States
should be officially aligned with the Protestant faith. Those who
challenged Article VI believed that it was important to exclude
Catholics and Muslims (and presumably atheists) from holding office
in the federal government. However, these concerns were rejected
when the Constitution received the necessary votes for ratification.[32]
The ratified Constitution not only prohibited religious tests for office

but it also made no reference to God or a divine being, and gave Congress no powers to assist religion. It asserted a breathtakingly secular vision of government and governing authority, especially when compared to prevailing English practices, the practices in the colonies, and the initial approach to church and state adopted by the state governments created immediately after Independence.

In the decade after Independence, some states rethought their position on religious establishments. The passage of the federal Constitution encouraged other states to change their practices. The South Carolina Constitution of 1778 had the longest provision of any constitution on religion. It declared that the Christian Protestant religion was "the established religion of the state" and that all Protestants sects were entitled to state assistance. Catholics and Jews were allowed to practice their faith but could receive no state support. But when South Carolina ratified a new constitution in 1790 it removed all religious tests for officeholders and deleted the intricate code of beliefs specified in Article 38 of the 1778 constitution.[33]

Debates about the proper relationship between church and state continued during the drafting of the Bill of Rights and the early experiences of governing under the new Constitution. Developments reinforced the movement away from establishment and conformity toward secularization and tolerance. Madison's initial draft of the Bill of Rights included two amendments relating to church and state. One applied against the national government that declared, "The civil rights of none shall be abridged on account of religious belief or worship, nor shall any national religion be established, nor shall the full and equal rights of conscience be in any manner or in any pretext, infringed." The other was designed to apply against the states, which declared, "No state shall violate the equal rights of conscience, nor the freedom of speech or of the press, nor the right of trial by jury in criminal cases." Although Madison wanted to prevent both the federal government and the states from penalizing citizens because of their religious affiliation, the final version of the Bill of Rights focused exclusively on limits imposed against the new federal government.[34]

Still, the final language of the Religion Clauses of the First Amendment—"*Congress shall make no law respecting an establishment of religion, or prohibiting the free exercise thereof*"—represented an extraordinary departure from a view of government that had dominated Europe since the days of the Emperor Constantine.

The sentiment was conveyed with lasting power by President George Washington in 1790, during the congressional debates over the Bill of Rights. Washington received an address by Moses Seixas, an official of the first Jewish congregation in Newport, Rhode Island, expressing gratitude to "behold a Government" in which "bigotry gives no sanction, to persecution no assistance—but generously affording to All liberty of conscience, and immunities of Citizenship: deeming every one, of whatever Nation, tongue, or language, equal parts of the great governmental Machine." Washington then penned a letter in response. The letter reassured those who fled religious tyranny that life in their new nation would be different, that religious "toleration" would give way to religious liberty, and that the government would not interfere with individuals in matters of conscience and belief. Quoting the Hebrew Bible, and echoing some of Moses Seixas's own language, he wrote in "The Letter to the Jews of Newport":

> Happily, the Government of the United States gives to bigotry no sanction, to persecution no assistance, requires only that they who live under its protections should demean themselves as good citizens, in giving it on all occasions their effectual support. . . . May the children of the stock of Abraham who dwell in this land continue to merit and enjoy the good will of the other

inhabitants—while every one shall sit in safety under his own vine and figtree, and there shall be none to make him afraid.[35]

Ten years later, the Danbury Baptist Association of Danbury, Connecticut, sent a letter to newly elected president Thomas Jefferson, expressing concern over the lack in their state constitution for protections against a religious establishment. "Our sentiments are uniformly on the side of religious liberty," they wrote, but the "religious privileges we enjoy (as a minor part of the State) we enjoy as favors granted, and not as inalienable rights." At the time, Connecticut was one of only three American states that still embraced the concept of official religious establishments. Jefferson's response, dated January 1, 1802, agreed that "religion is a matter which lies solely between man and God, that he owes account to none other for his faith or his worship." He went on: "I contemplate with sovereign reverence that act of the whole American people which declared that the legislature should 'make no law respecting an establishment of religion, or prohibiting the free exercise thereof,' thus building a wall of separation between church and State."[36]

WHAT THE FRAMERS DID AND DID NOT RESOLVE

While debates and controversies over the proper relationship between religion and government have persisted throughout American history, it is nevertheless important to recognize some fundamental issues that were resolved by the ratification of the Constitution and the subsequent Bill of Rights.

First, the new American republic rejected the centuries-old European practice of linking government authority to a favored religious tradition or sect. In America there would be no religion that had the kind of official status enjoyed by the Anglican Church in England or the Catholic Church in pre-revolutionary France. Despite the urgings of some figures who believed that the new republic should at least have a Christian identity, the framers of the 1789 Constitution rejected any religious test for office. The government would have a secular foundation, deriving its authority from the people rather than from its association with a particular religious tradition.

Second, while the government would have a secular identity, it would also recognize that the people would be free to exercise the religions of their choice. Unlike post-revolutionary France, there would be no effort to "secularize" the citizenry; instead, the practice of a diverse set of religions would be tolerated. This choice against secularization reflected the widely held view among Americans of that generation that religious sentiments were beneficial to society. Washington made the point in his Farewell Address when he cautioned against the view "that morality can be maintained without religion. Whatever may be conceded to the influence of refined education on minds of peculiar structure, reason and experience both forbid us to expect that national morality can prevail in exclusion of religious principle." However, the positive influence of religion on the body politic would arise from its presence in the private sphere, through the protection of religious liberty, rather than by virtue of its being a matter of regulation and direction by civil authority. Free exercise, rather than establishment, would provide the protection.[37]

These two decisions resolved many issues that had been matters of serious contention and controversy during the colonial period and the immediate period after independence was declared. But this "disestablishment/free exercise" approach also left unresolved a number of contentious questions.

For example, can a government that rejects establishment but values the presence of religion among the people provide non-denominational support for religious activity, such as tax breaks for religious institutions and leaders? When it offers benefits to institutions that promote secular government interests may it extend those benefits also to religious institutions, knowing that those resources can be used to support religious activity? Would it be appropriate for government officials, chosen without regard to a religious test for office, to nevertheless offer formal proclamations about the importance of religion? May it devise programs and allocate resources for the purpose of supporting and advancing presumptively non-denominational religious activity? When and to what extent can religion be part of official government activities?

In 1789, Washington issued a "Proclamation of a national day of Thanksgiving," premised on the view that "it is the duty of all nations to acknowledge the providence of Almighty God, to obey His will, to be grateful for His benefits, and humbly to implore His protection and favor." Jefferson, by contrast, openly denounced such a proclamation. Similarly, the first Congress hired Christian chaplains (of different denominations) to offer prayers but did so over the objections of James Madison, who argued that such a practice violated the Establishment Clause and also discriminated against religious groups such as Quakers and Catholics "who could scarcely be elected to office."[38]

Although the government was committed to tolerating a diverse range of religious practitioners, did that toleration extend only to the right to hold beliefs without punishment and engage in religious practices that did not contravene secular public policy, or was the scope of the protection broader than that? In particular, did religious practitioners have a right to be relieved of ordinary social duties that might interfere with their beliefs or behavioral obligations? It was Jefferson's view that religion would be protected in its "doctrines, discipline, or exercises" but that religious practitioners had no right to be excluded from "social duties." For example, an attempt to exempt the religiously scrupulous from military service, which was common in some state constitutions, failed in the new Congress. It was not until 1864 that Congress, for the first time, "mandated a religious exemption from a generally applicable secular law" by adopting an amendment declaring "that members of religious denominations, who shall, by oath or affirmation, declare that they are conscientiously opposed to the bearing of arms, and who are prohibited from doing so by the rules and articles of faith and practice of said religious denomination, shall, when drafted into the military service, be considered non-combatants, and shall be assigned by the Secretary of War to duty in the hospitals, or to the care of freedmen, or shall pay the sum of three hundred dollars to the benefit of the sick and wounded soldiers."[39] If one is tempted to offer some religious practitioners exemptions from the social duties imposed on everyone else, does that run the risk of forcing government officials to pick and choose among more or less "deserving" religious beliefs and practices, in a way that itself undermines the fundamental commitment to pass no laws respecting an establishment of religion?

The "disestablishment/free exercise" framework that was embedded in the American Constitution was exceptionally important—not to mention historically unprecedented. Even if subsequent historical debates revealed ongoing controversies and uncertainties, we should not underestimate the importance of these foundational decisions. What we experience as matters of great urgency and controversy actually reflect a relatively narrow spectrum of possible debates and battles about the role of religion in a political system. Even with waves of surging religious revivalism and periods of shameful religious bigotry, our debates took place within a set of assumptions that were not imaginable in the early 18th century.

Moreover, just as our credo that "all men are created equal" was corrupted, assaulted, and tormented by a history that assumed America was a country for the white race, so too was our secular republic corrupted, assaulted, and tormented by illegitimate assumptions that (nevertheless) America was really a Christian nation.[40] As we consider how to apply these traditions and legacies to contemporary issues, we should not be distracted by those aspects of our history that reflect our failures to live up to the aspirations of our founding documents. We have learned too much over two centuries about the norms of secular democracy, about tolerance for religious minorities, about respecting diverse views, and about the dangers of linking political fervor to religious fervor.

Justice Stevens once wrote, "It is our duty . . . to interpret the First Amendment's command that 'Congress make no law respecting an establishment of religion' not merely asking what those words meant to observers at the time of the founding, but instead by deriving from the Clause's text and history the broad principles that remain valid today."[41] We agree with this guidance on how we should proceed to interpret the Religion Clauses. The concerns of the framers led them to articulate broad principles that remain valid today. As we begin our review of contemporary debates we must also keep in mind how much we have improved our understanding of separating government from favored religions, and how our generation has a greater appreciation of the special challenges of maintaining religious liberty in our modern world—a world that has come to understand and appreciate religious traditions and practices that could not even be contemplated by the framers of the Constitution. It is to those challenges and opportunities that we now turn.

CHAPTER THREE

The Establishment Clause

In Defense of Separating Church and State

Congress shall make no law respecting an establishment of religion . . .

THE MEANING OF the Establishment Clause and whether it should be understood as creating a wall separating church and state is deeply contested along ideological grounds. While liberals generally favor separation of church and state, conservatives vehemently reject that and seek to allow more religious presence in government and more government support for religion. The shift in the ideological composition of the Supreme Court makes it likely that the latter view will triumph and that there will be dramatic changes in the law in this area.

There are strong emotions on both sides of this issue, as with so much concerning religion. In 2005, one of us (Erwin Chemerinsky) argued a case at the United States Supreme Court involving the constitutionality of the Ten Commandments monument that sits between the Texas State Capitol and the Texas Supreme Court.[1]

The monument is six feet high and three feet wide, and atop it in large letters it states, "I AM the LORD, thy God."

In the days before the argument at the Supreme Court, the case received a great deal of media attention.[2] Some of the reports mentioned that Chemerinsky was the attorney who would be arguing the case against the monument before the Court, and as a result, he received a large amount of hate mail. Some of it, in its viciousness, was shocking.

By itself, this showed that there are some people who care very deeply about having religious symbols on government property. But there were also more subtle lessons to be learned. The State of Texas was arguing to the Supreme Court that it wanted the Ten Commandments monument to remain because of the historical importance of the Ten Commandments as a source of law. This, though, was not at all the reason the people who were sending the hate mail wanted the monument there. They wanted the Ten Commandments there because it was a religious message and a religious symbol.

After all, it was not that long before that the chief justice of the Alabama Supreme Court, Roy Moore, was removed from office because of his insistence on keeping a two and a half ton Ten Commandments display in the Alabama State Courthouse.[3] He defied a court order to remove the Ten Commandments monument,[4] not because he thought it was an important historical symbol, but because it was a symbol of his religion. As he put it during his 2017 Senate campaign, "I want to see virtue and morality returned to our country and God is the only source of our law, liberty, and government."[5] On the other side of this heated debate, when Oklahoma installed a 4,800-pound Ten Commandments monument, a man rammed his car into it. He did the same thing after Arkansas decided to install a three-ton granite monument of the Ten Commandments.[6]

What underlies the debate—whether it is over the Ten Commandments at the Texas State Capitol grounds or the other examples—is the profound question of whether to have a secular government or whether to have a government that affiliates with and advances religion. As we discussed in Chapter 2, the framers resisted strong pressure to declare that the American republic would formally be associated with Christianity. There is no doubt that they intended to create a government that was formally secular, even if they also were committed to protecting the exercise of religion by individuals acting in their private capacity. They fought a war against a head of state who was also the head of a church, and they knew full well the dangers of that system and of sectarian conflict. But they did not resolve all questions or settle all disputes.

Was their vision satisfied merely by the prohibition against the formal establishment of a Church of the United States, or did it require also that government take no action that aligned itself with religious activities or symbols? Given that they wanted both a secular government and a people free to exercise religion, was it legitimate for the government to acknowledge and recognize the role of religion in the life of the people? If so, was that a tacit endorsement of religion, and if not, did that reflect an illegitimate hostility to religion? Could the government's use of religious symbols be justified as recognizing historical traditions and events without also conveying religious authority for the government? Can prayers or references to God be considered acceptable on the theory that they merely "solemnize" important occasions rather than act as inherently religious activities? In a world where the framers fought so hard against using tax dollars to support religious establishments, could it ever be legitimate for government funds to go to religious institutions?

In this chapter we examine the meaning of the Establishment Clause. We begin by describing competing theories of this constitutional provision. We then reject the idea that its meaning can be understood and defined based on history, given the long-standing practices of America's Protestant establishment (few of which are still defended as legitimate by judges and legal scholars) and America's history of animus against unfavored religions. In light of this we then defend our view that the Establishment Clause is best understood as requiring a wall that separates church and state. We conclude this chapter by applying this vision to some of the most important issues concerning the Establishment Clause, including the presence of religion in government activities and government support for religious institutions.

COMPETING THEORIES OF THE ESTABLISHMENT CLAUSE

There are three major competing approaches to the Establishment Clause. Each has adherents on the Court, and each is supported by a body of scholarly literature. The theory chosen very much determines the outcome in Establishment Clause cases.

Strict Separation

The first theory can be termed "strict separation." This approach says that to the greatest extent possible government and religion should be separated. The government should be, as much as possible, secular; religion should be entirely in the private realm of society. This theory is perhaps best described by Thomas Jefferson's metaphor that there should be a wall separating church and state.[7] As the Supreme Court declared in 1947 in *Everson v. Board of Education*, "The First Amendment has erected a wall between church and state. That wall must be kept high and impregnable."[8] The dissenting justices in this case not only agreed with this but wanted to go even further than the majority in restricting government aid to religion.[9]

Jefferson's famous words were uttered, as was Madison's Remonstrance, as part of a campaign against Virginia's renewing its tax to support the church. Justice Rutledge, in *Everson*, reviewed this history in describing the philosophy underlying the Establishment Clause: "The Amendment's purpose was not to strike merely at the official establishment of a single sect, creed or religion, outlawing only a formal relation such as had prevailed in England and some of the colonies. Necessarily it was to uproot all such relationships. But the object was broader than separating church and state in this narrow sense. It was to create a complete and permanent separation of the spheres of religious activity and civil authority by comprehensively forbidding every form of public aid or support for religion."[10]

A strict separation of church and state also is seen as necessary to protect religious liberty.[11] When religion becomes a part of government, separationists argue, there is inevitable coercion to participate in that faith. Those of different faiths and those who profess no religious beliefs are made to feel excluded and unwelcome when government and religion become intertwined. Moreover, government involvement with religion is inherently divisive in a country with so many different religions and many people who claim no religious beliefs at all.[12]

There are problems, though, with the strict separation approach, as there are for all of the theories. A complete prohibition of all government assistance to religion would threaten the free exercise of religion. For example, a refusal by the government to provide police, fire, or sanitation services for religious institutions obviously would infringe on free exercise. The failure of the government to provide chaplains for those in prison or in the military would infringe their free exercise of religion. Thus, a total wall separating church and state is impossible, and the issue becomes how to draw the appropriate line. Moreover, religion has traditionally been a part of many government activities, from the phrase "In God We Trust" on money (which was put there in 1956 as an expression of anti-communism) to the invocation before Supreme Court sessions, "God save this honorable Court."[13]

Neutrality Theory

A second major approach to the Establishment Clause says that the government must be neutral toward religion; that is, the government cannot favor religion over secularism or one religion over others. Professor Philip Kurland, an exponent of this approach to the Religion Clauses, wrote that "the clauses should be read as stating a single precept: that government cannot utilize religion as a standard for action or inaction because these clauses, read together as they should be, prohibit classification in terms of religion either to confer a benefit or to impose a burden."[14] Professor Douglas Laycock said that substantive neutrality means that "the religion clauses require government to minimize the extent to which it either encourages or discourages religious belief or disbelief, practice or nonpractice, observance or nonobservance."[15]

Several Supreme Court justices have advanced an "endorsement" test in evaluating the neutrality of a government's action. Under this approach, the government violates the Establishment Clause if it symbolically endorses a particular religion or if it generally endorses either religion or secularism. For example, Justice O'Connor has written that "every government practice must be judged in its unique circumstances to determine whether it constitutes an endorsement or disapproval of religion."[16]

Justice O'Connor explained the importance of such government neutrality: "As a theoretical matter, the endorsement test captures the essential command of the Establishment Clause, namely, that government must not make a person's religious beliefs relevant to his or her standing in the political community by conveying a message 'that religion or a particular religious belief is favored or preferred.' . . . If government is to be neutral in matters of religion, rather than showing either favoritism or disapproval towards citizens based on their personal religious choices, government cannot endorse the religious practices and beliefs of some citizens without sending a clear message to nonadherents that they are outsiders or less than full members of the political community."[17]

The difficulty is in determining what government actions constitute a "symbolic endorsement" of religion.[18] Several justices discussed this in 1995 in *Capitol Square Review and Advisory Board v. Pinette*.[19] The issue in *Pinette* was whether it was unconstitutional for the government to preclude the Ku Klux Klan from erecting a large Latin cross in the park across from the Ohio Statehouse. Although there was no majority opinion for the Court, seven justices voted that excluding the cross violated the Klan's free speech rights and that allowing it to be present would not violate the Establishment Clause. In the course of the Establishment Clause discussion, several of the justices addressed what constitutes an impermissible endorsement of religion.[20]

Justice O'Connor, in an opinion concurring in the judgment joined by Justices Souter and Breyer, concluded that the cross should be allowed because the reasonable observer would not perceive it as an endorsement of religion. O'Connor said that "where the government's operation of a public forum has the effect of endorsing religion, even if the governmental actor neither intends nor actively encourages that result, the Establishment Clause is violated."[21] Justice O'Connor said that a reasonable observer would not likely perceive the cross as being endorsed by the government because there was "a sign disclaiming government sponsorship or endorsement" and this would "remove doubt about the State approval of [the] religious message."[22]

O'Connor said that the symbolic endorsement test is applied "from the perspective of a hypothetical observer who is presumed to possess a certain level of information that all citizens might not share."[23] She said that the reasonable observer "must be deemed aware of the history and context of the community and forum in which the religious display appears [and] the general history of the place in which the cross is displayed. [An] informed member of the community will know how the public space in question has been used in the past."[24]

Justices Stevens and Ginsburg dissented and argued that there is an unconstitutional endorsement of religion if a reasonable person passing by would perceive government support for religion. Justice Stevens wrote: "If a reasonable person could perceive a government endorsement of religion from a private display, then the State may not allow its property to be used as a forum for that display. No less stringent rule can adequately protect non-adherents from a well-grounded perception that their sovereign supports a faith to which they do not subscribe."[25] Justice Stevens argued that Justice O'Connor's "'reasonable person' comes off as a well-schooled jurist, a being finer than the tort-law model. . . . [T]his enhanced tort-law standard is singularly out of place in the Establishment Clause context. It strips of constitutional protection every person whose knowledge happens to fall below some 'ideal' standard."[26]

Thus, three different approaches to the endorsement test were expressed in *Pinette*. Justice Scalia, writing for the plurality, rejected using the test at all where the issue is private speech on government property; indeed, Justice Scalia and other justices who take the accommodationist approach completely reject this test for determining whether there is a violation of the Establishment Clause. Justice O'Connor, writing for herself and Justices Souter and Breyer, said that the symbolic endorsement test should be applied from the perspective of the perceptions of a well-educated and well-informed observer. Justice Stevens, dissenting and joined by Justice Ginsburg, said that the symbolic endorsement test should look to the perceptions of the reasonable passerby.

The endorsement test is defended as a desirable approach to the Establishment Clause because it is a way of determining whether the government is neutral or whether it is favoring religion. A key purpose of the Establishment Clause is to prevent the government from making those who are not a part of the favored religion feel unwelcome. The endorsement test is seen as a way of assessing the likely perceptions of and reactions to government conduct.[27]

Those who criticize the symbolic endorsement test often focus on its ambiguity and indeterminacy.[28] People will perceive symbols in widely varying ways. The Court inevitably is left to make a subjective choice as to how people will perceive a particular symbol. Moreover, judges who are part of the dominant religion may be insensitive to how those of minority religions perceive particular symbols. At the same time, some argue that the endorsement test is too restrictive of government involvement with religion. Justice Kennedy, for example, said: "Either the endorsement test must invalidate scores of traditional practices recognizing the place religion holds in our culture, or it must be twisted and stretched to avoid inconsistency with practices we know to have been permitted in the past, while condemning similar practices with no greater endorsement effect simply by reason of their lack of historical antecedent. Neither result is acceptable."[29]

Accommodation

A third major theory can be termed an "accommodation" approach. Under this view, the Court should interpret the Establishment Clause to recognize the importance of religion in society and to accommodate its presence in government. Specifically, under the accommodation approach, the government violates the Establishment Clause only if it literally establishes a church, coerces religious participation, or favors one religion over others in its award of benefits. Justice Kennedy, for example, has said that "the Establishment Clause . . . guarantees at a minimum that a government may not coerce anyone to support or participate in religion or its exercise, or otherwise act in a way which establishes a [state] religion or religious faith, or tends to do so."[30] In fact, Justice Kennedy said that "barring all attempts to aid religion through government coercion goes far toward the attainment of [the] object [of the Establishment Clause]."[31] Justices taking this approach have described it in terms of the need for the government to treat religious beliefs and groups equally with nonreligious ones.[32] Whether termed accommodation or equality, the approach is the same: Government should accommodate religion by treating it the same as nonreligious beliefs and groups; the government violates the Establishment Clause only if it establishes a church, coerces religious participation, or favors some religions over others.

A key question under this approach concerns what constitutes government "coercion." Several justices discussed this in 1992 in *Lee v. Weisman*, where the Court declared unconstitutional clergy-delivered prayers at public school graduations.[33] Justice Kennedy, writing for the Court, found that such prayers are inherently coercive because there is great pressure on students to attend their graduation ceremonies and to not leave during the prayers.

Justice Blackmun, in an opinion joined by Justices Stevens and O'Connor, wrote to emphasize that the Establishment Clause can be violated even without coercion. He remarked that it "is not enough that the government refrain from compelling religious practices; it must not engage in them either."[34] Likewise, Justice Souter, joined by Justices Stevens and O'Connor, wrote separately to stress that coercion is sufficient for a finding of a violation of the Establishment

Clause, but it is not necessary; Establishment Clause violations exist without coercion if there is symbolic government endorsement of religion.

The dissenting opinion by Justice Scalia, joined by Chief Justice Rehnquist and Justices White and Thomas, advocated the accommodation approach but defined coercion much more narrowly than Justice Kennedy. Justice Scalia said that "the coercion that was a hallmark of historical establishments of religion was coercion of religious orthodoxy and of financial support by force of law and threat of penalty."[35]

In *Town of Greece v. Galloway*, Justice Thomas further elaborated on his view of "coercion."[36] The Court, in a 5–4 decision, in 2014, upheld the constitutionality of prayers before meetings of the Town Board, even though almost all of the prayers over a long period of time were delivered by Christian clergy. Justice Thomas concurred in the judgment, and in a part of the opinion joined by Justice Scalia, said that only "legal coercion"—a law demanding religious participation with legal consequences for violations—would violate the Establishment Clause. In other words, among the justices who take the accommodation approach, there is a disagreement over whether coercion can be found based on social pressures or whether it requires legal requirements for specific conduct.

Those who defend the accommodation approach argue that it best reflects the importance and prevalence of religion in American society. Professor Michael McConnell, an advocate of this view, said that it is desirable because it makes "religion . . . a welcome element in the mix of beliefs and associations present in the community. Under this view, the emphasis is placed on freedom of choice and diversity among religious opinion. The nation is understood not as secular but as pluralistic. Religion is under no special disability in public life; indeed, it is at least as protected and encouraged as any other form of belief and association—in some ways more so."[37]

Anything less than accommodation, it is argued, is unacceptable hostility to religion.

Opponents of the accommodation approach argue that, especially as defined by Justice Scalia, little ever will violate the Establishment Clause.[38] Nothing except the government creating its own church or by force of law requiring religious practices will offend the provision. Those disagreeing with this theory argue that the Establishment Clause also should serve to prevent the government from making those of other religions feel unwelcome and to keep the government from using its power and influence to advance religion or a particular religion. Justice O'Connor expressed this view when she wrote: "An Establishment Clause standard that prohibits only 'coercive' practices or overt efforts at government proselytization, but fails to take account of the numerous more subtle ways that government can show favoritism to particular beliefs or convey a message of disapproval to others, would not, in my view, adequately protect the religious liberty or respect the religious diversity of the members of our pluralistic political community. Thus, this Court has never relied on coercion alone as the touchstone of Establishment Clause analysis."[39] Justices O'Connor and Souter strongly objected that equality alone never has been regarded as the sole test of the Establishment Clause.

The Theories Applied: Examples

The importance of these three theories in determining the inquiry and the results in Establishment Clause cases is reflected in *Allegheny County v. Greater Pittsburgh ACLU*.[40] The case, decided in 1989, concerned two different religious displays. One was a crèche—a representation of the Nativity of Jesus—that was placed in a display case in a stairway in a county courthouse. The other display was in front of a government building and included a large Christmas tree, a large menorah (a candleholder used as part of the Chanukah celebration), and a sign saying that the city salutes liberty during the holiday season.

Three justices—Stevens, Brennan, and Marshall—took a strict separation approach and argued that both symbols should be deemed unconstitutional as violating the Establishment Clause. Justice Stevens said that the "Establishment Clause should be construed to create a strong presumption against the display of religious symbols on public property."[41]

Four justices—Kennedy, Rehnquist, Scalia, and White—took an accommodationist approach and would have allowed both symbols. Justice Kennedy wrote that "the principles of the Establishment Clause and our Nation's historic traditions of diversity and pluralism allow communities to make reasonable judgments respecting the accommodation or acknowledgement of holidays with both cultural and religious aspects."[42]

Justices Blackmun and O'Connor used a neutrality approach, specifically applying the symbolic endorsement test, and found that the menorah was constitutional, but the Nativity scene was unconstitutional. From their perspective, the menorah was permissible because it was accompanied by a Christian symbol (a Christmas tree) and a secular expression concerning liberty. But the Nativity scene was alone on government property and thus was likely to be perceived as symbolic endorsement for Christianity. Justice O'Connor concluded that "the city of Pittsburgh's combined holiday display had neither the purpose nor the effect of endorsing religion, but that Allegheny County's crèche display had such an effect."[43]

Thus, the result was 5 to 4 that the Nativity scene was unconstitutional but 6 to 3 that the menorah was permissible. The case clearly reflects the importance of the competing theories of the Establishment Clause.

The importance of the competing theories was very much in mind in briefing and arguing *Van Orden v. Perry*. As mentioned earlier, the Court considered the constitutionality of a six-foot-high, three-foot-wide Ten Commandments monument between the Texas State Capitol and the Texas Supreme Court.[44] It was clear that there were four justices—Rehnquist, Scalia, Kennedy, and Thomas—who were going to find the Ten Commandments monument to be constitutional. By their view, religious symbols on government property never violate the Establishment Clause because there is no coercion of religious participation. But it also was apparent that there would be three justices who would find the Ten Commandments monument to be unconstitutional: Stevens, Souter, and Ginsburg. They believe that religious symbols do not belong on government property. Thus, it was predictable that the case would turn on the two justices—O'Connor and Breyer—who would focus on whether it is an endorsement of religion.

Indeed, this is exactly what happened. Chief Justice Rehnquist wrote a plurality opinion, joined by Justices Scalia, Kennedy, and Thomas, that rejected an Establishment Clause challenge to the Ten Commandments monument. Justice Breyer, though, concurred in the judgment and voted to uphold the monument's constitutionality. He expressly said that he applied the symbolic endorsement test but concluded that there was not symbolic endorsement in this case because of the presence of many other secular monuments on the Texas State Capitol grounds and because the monument had been there for over 40 years without challenge. Justices Stevens, O'Connor, Souter, and Ginsburg dissented and would have found the monument unconstitutional as a violation of the Establishment Clause.

In *Allegheny County* in 1989 and in *Van Orden v. Perry* in 2005, no theory commanded support from a majority of the justices. However, with changes in the composition of the Court, it is possible—indeed likely—that a majority of the justices now take this accommoda-tionist approach. In its most recent Establishment Clause case, *American Legion v. American Humanist Association*, in 2019, the Court considered the constitutionality of a 40-foot cross that sits on public property in Prince George's County, Maryland.[45] The cross was erected in 1920 as a memorial to those who died in military service in World War I.

The Court in a 7–2 decision rejected the constitutional chal-lenge. Justice Alito wrote, in part for the majority and in part for a plurality, and stressed that although a cross is a religious symbol, it also has other non-religious significance, including as a memorial for war dead. He explained: "The cross came into widespread use as a symbol of Christianity by the fourth century, and it retains that meaning today. But there are many contexts in which the symbol has also taken on a secular meaning. Indeed, there are instances in which its message is now almost entirely secular."[46] Echoing Justice Breyer's opinion in *Van Orden*, Justice Alito stressed that the monu-ment long had been present and to remove it would be hostility to religion. Justice Alito declared: "The passage of time gives rise to a strong presumption of constitutionality."[47]

Justice Thomas concurred in the judgment and repeated his view that the Establishment Clause does not apply to state and local gov-ernments at all. He stated, as he has expressed in the past, "The text and history of this Clause suggest that it should not be incorporated against the States."[48] He believes that the Establishment Clause was meant to keep the federal government from establishing a national church to rival state churches, not to create individual rights. Under this approach, a state or local government *never* would violate the Establishment Clause; even if it declared an official state religion it would not offend the First Amendment.

Justice Gorsuch concurred in the judgment and argued that no one has standing to challenge a religious symbol on government property.[49] He said that no one is sufficiently injured to permit a suit in federal court. He concluded that "suits like this one should be dismissed for lack of standing."[50] This, of course, would mean that the government can put any religious symbol it wants on any piece of government property and no federal court could stop it because under Justice Gorsuch's view no one ever would have standing to challenge this.

Justice Kavanaugh concurred and wrote separately to say that he believed that the Court had overruled the test from *Lemon v. Kurtzman*, a position long taken by those who advocate the accommodationist approach to the Establishment Clause.[51] He made clear that religious symbols on government property do not offend the Constitution: "The practice of displaying religious memorials, particularly religious war memorials, on public land is not coercive and is rooted in history and tradition."[52]

Only Justices Ginsburg and Sotomayor dissented.[53] Justice Ginsburg expressed the view that a cross is the quintessential Christian religious symbol and the display of a 40-foot cross on public property violates the Establishment Clause. She wrote: "By maintaining the Peace Cross on a public highway, the Commission elevates Christianity over other faiths, and religion over nonreligion. Memorializing the service of American soldiers is an 'admirable and unquestionably secular' objective. But the Commission does not serve that objective by displaying a symbol that bears 'a starkly sectarian message.'"[54]

From this case, and other recent decisions such as *Town of Greece v. Galloway*, it seems that there are now five justices—Roberts, Thomas (who does not believe that the Establishment Clause applies to the states at all), Alito, Gorsuch, and Kavanaugh—who take the accommodationist approach. For them, the government will be found to violate the Establishment Clause only when it coerces religious participation or discriminates among religions in the distribution of benefits. Rarely will the government be deemed to infringe this part of the First Amendment. There are likely two justices—Breyer and Kagan—who take the neutrality, or endorsement, approach. And there are now just two justices—Ginsburg and Sotomayor—who take the strict separationist view of the Establishment Clause.

HISTORY PROVIDES NO ANSWER

It is tempting to try to decide among these approaches and determine the meaning of the Establishment Clause from history. Indeed, as we argue in Chapter 2, we think it is clear that overall the framers of the Constitution wanted a secular government and favored what today we would label a "separationist" approach to the Establishment Clause. But as we indicated at the beginning of this chapter, history does not provide an answer to the specific questions that arise in applying the Establishment Clause. Asking what the framers would have allowed in terms of giving computers to parochial schools is a meaningless question when education is so vastly different today than in 1791. The many problems with originalism as a theory of constitutional interpretation are familiar.[55] We think that Justice Robert Jackson got it right, albeit in another context, when he said, "Just what our forefathers did envision, or would have envisioned had they foreseen modern conditions, must be divined from materials almost as enigmatic as the dreams Joseph was called upon to interpret for Pharaoh."[56] Research will reveal little more than competing quotations about religion that each side cites to support its position.

Justice Brennan expressed this well in speaking about the Religion Clauses when he stated: "A too literal quest for the advice of the Founding Fathers upon the issues of these cases seems to me futile and misdirected for several reasons. . . . [T]he historical record is at best ambiguous, and statements can readily be found to support either side of the proposition."[57] Yet justices on all sides of the issue continue to invoke history and the framers' intent to support their position. Chief Justice Rehnquist has remarked that "the true meaning of the Establishment Clause can only be seen in its history."[58] In the Supreme Court's decision in *Rosenberger v. Rector and Visitors of the University of Virginia*, which concerned whether a public university could deny student activity funds to a religious group, both Justice Thomas in a concurring opinion and Justice Souter dissenting focused at length on James Madison's views of religious freedom and government aid to religious institutions.[59]

As Professor Laurence Tribe has cogently summarized, there were at least three main views of religion among key framers.[60]

> At least three distinct schools of thought ... influenced the drafters of the Bill of Rights: first, the evangelical view (associated primarily with Roger Williams) that "worldly corruptions ... might consume the churches if sturdy fences against the wilderness were not maintained"; second, the Jeffersonian view that the church should be walled off from the state in order to safeguard secular interests (public and private) "against ecclesiastical depredations and incursions"; and, third, the Madisonian view that religious and secular interests alike would be advanced best by diffusing and decentralizing power so as to assure competition among sects rather than dominance by any one.[61]

These are quite distinct views of the proper relationship between religion and the government. Roger Williams was primarily concerned that government involvement with religion would corrupt and undermine religion, whereas Thomas Jefferson had the opposite fear: that religion would corrupt and undermine the government. James Madison saw religion as one among many types of factions that existed and that needed to be preserved. He wrote that "in a free government the security for civil rights must be the same as that for religious rights. It consists in the one case in the multiplicity of interests, and the other in the multiplicity of sects. The degree of security in both cases will depend on the number of interests and sects."[62]

The problem of using history in interpreting the Religion Clauses is compounded by the enormous changes in the country since the First Amendment was adopted. The country is far much more religiously heterogeneous today than it was in 1791. Justice Brennan observed that "our religious composition makes us a vastly more diverse people than were our forefathers. They knew differences chiefly among Protestant sects. Today the nation is far more heterogeneous religiously, including as it does substantial minorities not only of Catholics and Jews but as well of those who worship according to no version of the Bible and those who worship no God at all."[63]

Also, as discussed later, a significant number of cases involving the Establishment Clause have arisen in the context of religious activities in connection with schools.[64] But public education, as it exists now, did not exist when the Bill of Rights was ratified, and it is inherently difficult to apply the framers' views to situations that they could not have imagined. Justice Brennan also remarked that "the structure of American education has greatly changed since the First Amendment was adopted. In the context of our modern emphasis upon public education available to all citizens, any views of the eighteenth century as to whether the exercises at bar are an 'establishment' offer little aid to decision."[65] Nonetheless, debates about history and the framers' intent are likely to remain a key aspect of decisions concerning the Religion Clauses. Members of the Supreme Court who follow an originalist philosophy of constitutional interpretation believe that the Constitution's meaning is to be ascertained solely from its text and from its framers' intent. Also, the divergence of views among the framers, and the abstractness with which they were stated, makes it possible for those on all sides of the debate to invoke history in support of their positions. Those who favor strict separation can point to the words of Jefferson and Madison; those who favor accommodation can point to the religious content of George Washington's Thanksgiving Proclamation and the presence of religion in government activities early in American history. But in the end, each side is left with examples and quotations, but there is no definitive answer based on history, even assuming that history should be determinative in resolving contemporary constitutional questions.

IN DEFENSE OF SEPARATION

We think that Thomas Jefferson got it right when he coined the phrase that there should be "a wall of separation between church and state"[66]—a wall that the Supreme Court later declared should be both "high and impregnable."[67] It is interesting that when the Supreme Court in 1947 held that the Establishment Clause applied to state and local governments, all nine justices then on the Court endorsed this notion that there should be a wall separating church and state.[68]

There are many reasons that this is the best approach to the Establishment Clause.

First, although history cannot provide definitive answers to the contemporary controversies, there is no doubt that the founding generation was concerned above all with making sure that the government was not at all involved in religious activity. They were well aware of the political instabilities that were associated with religious practitioners believing that government might be a partner in their religious endeavors. To the best of their ability they ensured that the American republic would claim no authority from religion, would have no jurisdiction to legislate on matters of religion, and would have no religious tests for office. Many of them had participated in some of the most important developments leading to a vision of a secular government that should be viewed as having nothing interesting to say about religion, other than that it would protect the rights of individuals in their private capacity to believe and worship as they saw fit based on the commands of their private conscience. It was fine for people to be religious if they so chose, but it was not the role of government to influence the people one way or the other. The responsibilities of the public magistrate were fundamentally different from the responsibilities of the clergy. This was their overriding accomplishment and their most revolutionary break from all previous understandings of the relationship between governments and religion in the political traditions with which they were familiar.

Second, and relatedly, the separation approach is the best way of ensuring that we can all feel that it is "our" government, whatever our religion or lack of religion. If government becomes aligned with a particular religion or religions, or with some overarching religious traditions (e.g., Judeo-Christian) over others (Hindu or Santiera), those of other beliefs will be made to feel like outsiders, inherently alienated from the government that claims to represent us all. Justice O'Connor captured this better than anyone in her writings for the Court. She said that the Establishment Clause is there to make sure that none of us is led to feel that we are insiders or outsiders when it comes to our government. She wrote: "Endorsement [of religion by the government] sends a message to nonadherents that they are outsiders, and not full members of the political community, and an accompanying message to adherents that they are insiders."[69]

If our government becomes aligned with religion or a particular religion, some of us are made to feel that we just do not belong in that place. If there were a large Latin cross atop a city hall, those who were not part of religions that accept the cross as a religious symbol would feel that it was not "their" city government. Both of us grew up mindful that we were Jewish in a Christian-dominated political system and we believed we were as entitled to the government's respect as those who had their Christmas holidays formally recognized in our school's calendar, even though our Jewish holidays were not. In the same way, how would one who does not accept God, or one who does not believe that there is one God, feel about walking into the Texas Supreme Court or the Texas State Capitol and seeing "I am the Lord, thy God," and seeing underneath it, "Thou shalt have no other gods before me"? If we want all citizens to feel that the government is open for everyone we need our government to be strictly secular—respectful of all, without signaling an alliance, public or secret, with just some.

A third important reason to favor separation is that it is wrong to tax people to support the religion of others. James Madison captured this best in Virginia, where he talked about why he believed that it was, in his words, "immoral" to tax people to support religions in which they did not believe.[70] Each of us has our own religion, or maybe we decided that we do not have any religion, but should our tax dollars go to advance a religion in which we do not believe? What if it is a religion that teaches things that we find abhorrent? Certainly we have the right to give our money to support any religion or any cause we want, but it is wrong to be coerced to give our tax dollars to religions we do not believe in. That is why separation is best: it allows people to choose how to spend their money rather than permitting the government to use it against their own wishes. This does not deny that there are line drawing issues with regard to funding, some of which we discuss later. Not providing police and fire protection to houses of worship would present serious free exercise clause issues. But that does not mean that the government paying for everything else—even salaries for clergy—should be permissible.

A fourth reason that separation is best is that it prevents the coercion that is inherent when the government becomes aligned with religion. World history, to say nothing of the history of this country, shows us that when the government becomes aligned with religion, people feel coerced to participate.[71] As the Court explained in *Engel v. Vitale*, "the indirect coercive pressure upon religious minorities to conform to the prevailing officially approved religion is plain."[72]

This is especially the case in the context of public schools. Certainly, this is why the Supreme Court has repeated for forty-five years that prayer, even voluntary prayer, does not belong in public schools.[73] Students who are from minority religions, or who have no religious upbringing, feel enormous social pressure to participate in the prayers of their classmates rather than risk being ostracized and ridiculed. This was exactly Justice Kennedy's point in *Lee v. Weisman*. Once the government becomes aligned with religion, coercion becomes so easy. We have seen this at public universities. Cadets at the Air Force Academy talk movingly about being forced to participate in Christian religious ceremonies, even if they are not Christians.[74] This is the danger if church and state are not separate.

A fifth reason that separation is the best theory is to protect religion. America is the most religious and religiously diverse nation in the developed Western world, and to a large extent this is because people understand that the government will play no favorites, thus allowing all people of faith to worship without fear or oppression. Roger Williams, a co-founder of Rhode Island, talked about this prior to the drafting of the Establishment Clause.[75] He wanted to separate church and state not to safeguard the state from religion, but to protect religion from the state. The reality is that the more the government becomes involved in religion, the more the government will regulate religion and, consequently, the greater the danger is to religion. There is also the danger of trivializing religion. To say that a cross is just there for secular purposes—as Justice Alito said in *American Legion v. American Humanist Association*—ignores how important the cross is as a religious symbol.

Separation is not hostile to religion.[76] Of course, any enforcement of the Establishment Clause will be seen by those who want a religious presence as hostility to religion. But that view begs the question and assumes that a religious presence in government is permissible. If the Constitution is seen as requiring separation of church and state, excluding religion is enforcing the view that the place for religion should be in the private realm. Our government should be secular—for the sake of a less turbulent political system and for the sake of a diverse set of religious practitioners seeking a political context where their personal religious convictions will be respected.

APPLICATIONS

What would it mean for the Court to follow the separation approach? Consider several examples: prayers at government activities, religious symbols on government property, and government aid to religious institutions.

Prayer

We believe the Supreme Court has gotten it right in holding that prayer in public schools—even voluntary school prayer—violates the Constitution. Few Supreme Court decisions have been as controversial as those that declared prayers and Bible readings in public schools unconstitutional. The Supreme Court has invalidated prayer in public schools, including voluntary prayers led by instructors and a government-mandated moment of "silence" for "meditation or silent prayer." The Court also has followed this reasoning to invalidate clergy-delivered prayers at public school graduations.

Engel v. Vitale, in 1962, was the initial Supreme Court case holding prayers in public schools to be unconstitutional.[77] *Engel* invalidated a school policy of having a "non-denominational prayer," composed by the state's Board of Regents, recited at the beginning of each school day. The prayer was: "Almighty God, we acknowledge our dependence upon Thee, and we beg Thy blessings upon us, our parents, our teachers and our Country."[78]

The Court, in an opinion by Justice Black, said that "there can be no doubt that New York's state prayer program officially establishes the religious beliefs embodied in the Regents' prayer. . . . Neither the fact that the prayer may be denominationally neutral nor the fact that its observance on the part of the students is voluntary can serve to free it from the limitations of the Establishment Clause."[79] The Court explained that the Establishment Clause rests on the "belief that a union of government and religion tends to destroy government and to degrade religion. . . . The Establishment Clause thus stands as an expression of principle on the part of the Founders of our Constitution that religion is too personal, too sacred, too holy, to permit its 'unhallowed perversion' by a civil magistrate."[80] It should be noted that the so-called denominationally neutral prayer was still exclusive of a tremendous range of religious beliefs and practices. Hindus and Native Americans (for example) could never consider the language of the prayer as genuinely neutral with respect to America's modern diversity of religious views and practices.

The Court emphasized the unconstitutionality of the government writing prayers and directing that they be read within the public schools. Justice Black expressly rejected the argument that forbidding prayers constituted hostility to religion: "It is neither sacrilegious nor antireligious to say that each separate government in this country should stay out of the business of writing or sanctioning official prayers and leave that purely religious function to the people themselves and to those the people choose to look to for religious guidance."[81]

A year later, in *Abington School District v. Schempp*, the Court declared unconstitutional a state's law and a city's rule that required the reading, without comment, at the beginning of each school day of verses from the Bible and the recitation of the Lord's Prayer by students in unison.[82] Although *Schempp*, unlike *Engel*, did not involve a state-composed prayer, the laws requiring Bible reading and reciting of the Lord's Prayer were deemed to violate the Establishment Clause. The Court emphasized that these religious exercises were prescribed as part of the curricular activities of students, conducted in school buildings, and supervised by teachers.

The Court distinguished studying the Bible in a literature or comparative religion course, which would be permissible. The Court said that "the exercises here do not fall into those categories. They are religious exercises, required by the States in violation of the command of the First Amendment that the Government maintain strict neutrality, neither aiding nor opposing religion."[83]

In *Wallace v. Jaffree*, decided in 1985, the Court followed *Engel* and *Schempp* and declared unconstitutional an Alabama law that authorized a moment of silence in public schools for "meditation or voluntary prayer."[84] The legislative history of the law was clear that its purpose was to reintroduce prayer into the public schools.[85] The Court said that the record was "unambiguous" that the law "was not motivated by any clearly secular purpose—indeed, the statute had *no* secular purpose."[86]

In 1992, the Court reaffirmed and extended the ban on prayers in the public schools in *Lee v. Weisman*.[87] In *Lee*, the Court declared unconstitutional clergy-delivered prayers at public school graduations. Justice Kennedy, writing for the Court, said that cases such as *Engel, Schempp*, and *Wallace* were controlling and indistinguishable.

He said: "The controlling precedents as they relate to prayer and religious exercise in primary and secondary public schools compel the holding here. . . . The State's involvement in the school prayers challenged today violates these central principles [of the Establishment Clause.]"[88] The school decided that there should be a religious invocation and benediction, chose a clergy member to perform the prayers, and gave instructions concerning them.

Justice Kennedy stressed the inherent coercion in allowing prayer at graduations. Although no student was required to attend graduation, it is an important event in a person's life and students likely feel psychological pressure not to absent themselves during the prayer. He wrote that there "are heightened concerns with protecting freedom of conscience from subtle coercive pressure in the elementary and secondary public schools. [What] to most believers may seem nothing more than a reasonable request that the nonbeliever respect their religious practices, in a school context may appear to the nonbeliever or dissenter to be an attempt to employ the machinery of the State to enforce a religious orthodoxy."[89] All of these points would be obvious if the language and traditions used during these moments reflected the spiritual practices of religious sects that were far removed from our traditional Protestant establishment.

Justice Blackmun, in a concurring opinion joined by Justices Stevens and O'Connor, emphasized that prayers in public schools are unconstitutional even in the absence of coercion. He said that "it is not enough that the government restrain from compelling religious practices: it must not engage in them either. . . . Our decisions have gone beyond prohibiting coercion."[90] Likewise, Justice Souter, in a concurring opinion joined by Justices Stevens and O'Connor, argued that the Establishment Clause is violated by prayers at public school events regardless of whether there is a finding of coercion.

But Justice Scalia, joined by Chief Justice Rehnquist and Justices White and Thomas, vehemently dissented and disagreed with the view that there was anything coercive about a clergy-delivered prayer at a public school graduation. Scalia said that even if a student did feel subtly coerced to stand during the prayer, this was acceptable because maintaining "respect for the religious observance of others is a fundamental civic virtue that government can and should cultivate."[91] For Scalia, the prohibition of prayer constitutes impermissible hostility to religion. He wrote: "The reader has been told much in this case about the personal interest of [the plaintiffs], and very little about the personal interests on the other side. They are not inconsequential. Church and state would not be such a difficult subject if religion were, as the Court apparently thinks it to be, some purely personal avocation that can be indulged entirely in secret, like pornography, in the privacy of one's room. For most believers it is not that, and has never been. . . . But the longstanding American tradition of prayer at official ceremonies displays with unmistakable clarity that the Establishment Clause does not forbid the government to accommodate it."[92] This view would allow explicitly sectarian prayers at any government event so long as no one was legally forced to participate. We regard this as anathema to how the Establishment Clause should be interpreted.

Subsequent Supreme Court decisions concerning prayers in the public schools continue to find that such activity is impermissible at official school activities, particularly where the school encourages and facilitates prayer. In *Santa Fe Independent School District v. Doe*, in 2000, the Supreme Court, in a 6-to-3 decision, held that student-delivered prayers at high school football games violate the Establishment Clause.[93] A public high school in Texas had a tradition of having a student deliver a prayer before varsity football games. After this was challenged in litigation, the school adopted a policy where students would hold two elections; one was to decide whether to have invocations before football games and, if so, the second was to select the student to give the invocation.

Justice Stevens, writing for the Court, emphasized that the school had encouraged and facilitated the prayer at an official school event. The school claimed that the student prayers were private speech, but the Court emphatically disagreed. Justice Stevens explained: "We are not persuaded that the pregame invocations should be regarded as 'private speech.' These invocations are authorized by a government policy and take place on government property at government-sponsored school-related events."[94] The Court noted how the school encouraged the delivery of prayers, both in its official policies and in its traditional support for prayer at football games. The result is both actual and likely perceived government endorsement of religion. Justice Stevens stated: "The actual or perceived endorsement of the message, moreover, is established by factors beyond just the text of the policy. Once the student speaker is selected and the message composed, the invocation is then delivered to a large audience assembled as part of a regularly scheduled, school-sponsored function conducted on school property. The message is broadcast over the school's public address system, which remains subject to the control of school officials."[95]

Justice Stevens also noted the coercive aspects of the school's policy in that many students—football players, band members, cheerleaders—were required to be present in order to receive academic credit, as well as the benefits from participating in an extracurricular activity. The Court said that forcing students to choose between attending the game and avoiding religion violated the Establishment Clause: "The Constitution, moreover, demands that the school may not force this difficult choice upon these students for it is a tenet of the First Amendment that the State cannot require one of its citizens to forfeit his or her rights and benefits as the price of resisting conformance to state-sponsored religious practice."[96]

It is notable that Justice Stevens's majority opinion avoided choosing among the theories of the Establishment Clause; he explained why the prayers failed scrutiny under any of the leading tests. The dissent, written by Chief Justice Rehnquist, saw the exclusion of prayer as undue hostility to religion. He wrote: "But even more disturbing than its holding is the tone of the Court's opinion; it bristles with hostility to all things religious in public life. Neither the holding nor the tone of the opinion is faithful to the meaning of the Establishment Clause, when it is recalled that George Washington himself, at the request of the very Congress which passed the Bill of Rights, proclaimed a day of 'public thanksgiving and prayer,' to be observed by acknowledging with grateful hearts the many and signal favors of Almighty God."[97] Chief Justice Rehnquist's dissent thus is similar to Justice Scalia's lament in dissent in *Lee v. Weisman* that the Court was wrongly ignoring the interests of those who want prayer. It is a view that would impose no limits on prayer at government functions, including in schools, so long as no one was punished for failing to participate in the prayers.

Engel, Schempp, Wallace, Lee, and *Doe* establish that prayer—even if voluntary, non-denominational, or silent—is impermissible in public schools.[98] The cases embody the view that government-directed prayer is inherently religious activity and therefore does not belong in public schools. Students are required by compulsory attendance laws to be present, and even voluntary prayers are coercive.[99] Students who do not believe in religion or are part of religions that do not believe in prayers are inherently made to feel unwelcome and to be outsiders when prayer occurs in the classroom. Yet critics of the Court's decisions argue that prayer should be allowed in schools because of its importance in students' lives and because it is not coercive so long as it is voluntary. Former Solicitor General Erwin Griswold said: "No compulsion is put upon him. He need not participate. But he, too, has the opportunity to be tolerant. He allows the majority of the group to follow their own tradition, perhaps coming to understand and to respect what they feel is significant to them."[100]

We believe that under any of the theories of the Establishment Clause, prayer in public schools should be deemed to violate the Establishment Clause: there is coercion, even without sanctions, to participate; it is a government endorsement of religion; and it is a religious presence in government that does not belong. If the presumptively neutral practices involved prayer rugs pointed in the direction of Mecca, or Native American offerings to nature, the point would need no further elaboration to those who currently assume their practices reflect the neutral baseline rather than the preferred tradition.

By contrast, we strongly disagree with the Court's decisions that have allowed prayer at government meetings. In *Marsh v. Chambers*, the Supreme Court upheld the constitutionality of a state legislature employing a Presbyterian minister for 18 years to begin each session with a prayer.[101] The Nebraska legislature had employed Robert E. Palmer, a Presbyterian minister, since 1965 to open each legislative day with a prayer. The Court upheld this as constitutional because of the long history and tradition of religious invocations before legislative sessions.

Chief Justice Burger, writing for the Court in 1983, said that "the opening of sessions of legislative and other deliberative public bodies with prayer is deeply embedded in the history and tradition of this country. From colonial times through the founding of the Republic and ever since, the practice of legislative prayer has coexisted with the principles of disestablishment and religious freedom."[102] After reviewing this history in detail, Burger concluded that "this unique history leads us to accept the interpretation of the First Amendment draftsmen who saw no real threat to the Establishment Clause arising from a practice of prayer similar to that now challenged."[103] The Court said: "In light of the unambiguous and unbroken history of more than 200 years, there can be no doubt that the practice of opening legislative sessions with prayer has become part of the fabric of our society. . . . Nor is the compensation of the chaplain from public funds a reason to invalidate the Nebraska Legislature's chaplaincy: Remuneration is grounded in historic practice initiated . . . by the same Congress that drafted the Establishment Clause of the First Amendment."[104]

The dissent, though, stressed that the purpose of legislative prayers and paying a minister seems obviously to advance religion.[105] Paying a minister, from one faith, for 18 years from public funds clearly seems to have the effect of advancing that religion and of entangling government with religion.[106] Historical practice should not justify a constitutional violation. Segregation of schools or the prohibition of same-sex marriage were not made permissible by long historical practice.

The Court returned to the issue of prayers before legislative sessions in 2014 in *Town of Greece v. Galloway*, which held that it does not violate the Establishment Clause for a town board to begin virtually every meeting over a 10-year period with a prayer by a Christian minister.[107] The Town of Greece is a suburb of Rochester, New York, of about 100,000 people. Its town board opened meetings with a moment of silence until 1999 when the town supervisors initiated a policy change. The town began inviting ministers to begin meetings each month with a prayer. From 1999 to 2007, the town invited exclusively Christian ministers, most of whom gave explicitly Christian prayers.

In 2007, complaints were made to the town board about this and for four months clergy from other religions were invited. But then for the next 18 months, the town board reverted to inviting only Christian clergy and their prayers were almost always Christian in their content.

The Court, in a 5–4 decision, held that the Town of Greece did not violate the Establishment Clause. The Court stressed the long history of prayers before legislative sessions, including explicitly Christian prayers, and said that *Marsh* "teaches . . . that the Establishment Clause must be interpreted 'by reference to historical practices and understandings.'"[108] The Court said that for it to require non-sectarian prayers would put the government and the courts unduly in the position of monitoring the content of the prayers delivered by others: "To hold that invocations must be nonsectarian would force the legislatures that sponsor prayers and the courts that are asked to decide these cases to act as supervisors and censors of religious speech, a rule that would involve government in religious matters to a far greater degree than is the case under the town's current practice of neither editing or approving prayers in advance nor criticizing their content after the fact."[109]

The Court expressed great deference to the government in having prayers before legislative sessions and held: "Absent a pattern of prayers that over time denigrate, proselytize, or betray an impermissible government purpose, a challenge based solely on the content of a prayer will not likely establish a constitutional violation."[110]

Justice Kagan wrote a dissent, which was joined by Justices Ginsburg, Breyer, and Sotomayor.[111] The dissent found that the town board violated the Establishment Clause by inviting virtually only Christian clergy over a long period of time who delivered explicitly Christian prayers. Justice Kagan wrote: "The Town of Greece's prayer practices violate that norm of religious equality— the breathtakingly generous constitutional idea that our public institutions belong no less to the Buddhist or Hindu than to the Methodist or Episcopalian."[112] Justice Kagan explicitly distinguished *Marsh v. Chambers*: "The practice at issue here differs from the one sustained in *Marsh* because Greece's town meetings involve participation by ordinary citizens, and the invocations given—directly to those citizens—were predominantly sectarian in content. Still more, Greece's Board did nothing to recognize religious diversity: In arranging for clergy members to open each meeting, the

Town never sought (except briefly when this suit was filed) to involve, accommodate, or in any way reach out to adherents of non-Christian religions. So month in and month out for over a decade, prayers steeped in only one faith, addressed toward members of the public, commenced meetings to discuss local affairs and distribute government benefits. In my view, that practice does not square with the First Amendment's promise that every citizen, irrespective of her religion, owns an equal share in her government."[113]

The notion of a wall separating church and state is that our government should be secular. The Town of Greece's practice is the antithesis of such separation of church and state. It was the government beginning meetings over a long period of time with prayers of one religion.

Even under the more relaxed approach to the Establishment Clause which finds a violation only when there is government endorsement of religion, the Town of Greece acted unconstitutionally. As the Second Circuit concluded, the town's prayer practice had unconstitutionally affiliated the town with Christianity. The Establishment Clause of the First Amendment is violated when a town so clearly links itself to Christianity, by inviting only Christian clergy to deliver prayers for a long period of time and those prayers being explicitly Christian.

In fact, even under the coercion test—unless it is limited to legal coercion as Justice Thomas advocated—the town acted unconstitutionally. The prayers were delivered to an audience of local citizens, including both children and adults, who attended meetings at the town board's invitation or direction. Children's athletic teams were invited to be publicly honored for their successes, police officers and their families attended to participate in oath-of-office ceremonies, people came to speak to the board about local issues of great personal importance, and would-be business owners came to request zoning permits from the board. All of these people—Christians and non-Christians—were asked to stand and bow their heads for many of these prayers. But Muslims, Jews, and non-believers cannot in good conscience participate in a prayer to Jesus Christ, and doing so should not be the price of civic participation.

Religious Symbols on Government Property

As previously expressed, our view is that religious symbols do not belong on government property. We understand the argument that even a secular government should not separate itself from a religious people, but in most cases the advocacy in favor of the use of religious symbols reflects an underlying desire to maintain historical practices that endorsed particular religious practices to the exclusion of others rather than secular efforts to honor and acknowledge historical and traditional aspects of the American experience. Roy Moore was no secular historian or anthropologist.

We thus are critical of the many Supreme Court cases that have permitted this. Because of the division among the justices among the three theories of the Establishment Clause, the result has been that the Supreme Court has ruled that Nativity scenes, menorahs, and other religious symbols are allowed on government property as long as they do not convey symbolic government endorsement for religion or for a particular religion. And as we discussed earlier, with five current justices taking the accommodation approach, the Court in the future will likely find no religious symbols on government property to be unconstitutional.

In *Lynch v. Donnelly*, the Supreme Court upheld the constitutionality of a Nativity scene in a park.[114] The Christmas display included, among other things, a Santa Claus house, reindeer pulling Santa's sleigh, a Christmas tree, hundreds of colored lights, and a crèche. All of the display was owned by the city and placed in a park maintained by a not-for-profit organization.

The Court, in an opinion by Chief Justice Burger, found that the Nativity scene did not violate the Establishment Clause. Burger began by reviewing the many ways in which religion has traditionally been a part of government, from President George Washington's Thanksgiving Day proclamation to the slogan "In God We Trust" on currency. Burger concluded that the Nativity scene was permissible because it was motivated by a secular purpose: celebrating Christmas. He wrote: "The narrow question is whether there is a secular purpose for Pawtucket's display of the crèche. The display is sponsored by the city to celebrate the Holiday and to depict the origins of that Holiday. These are legitimate secular purposes."[115]

Yet from the perspective of both Christians and non-Christians this view of the Nativity scene seems wrong. As Justice Brennan noted in dissent, the crèche is a "re-creation of an event that lies at the heart of the Christian faith."[116] For Christians, it is a basic religious symbol and it is likely perceived that way by non-Christians as well. Our position is that a profoundly religious symbol, like a Nativity scene or a cross, does not belong on government property. For most people this would be an incredibly easy point to accept if, for example, we were debating government sponsorship of the Star and Crescent symbol rather than crosses and crèches.

In *Allegheny County v. Greater Pittsburgh ACLU*, which we describe earlier, the Court recognized the inherently religious nature of the Nativity scene.[117] This case, decided in 1989, involved two December holiday displays: One was a crèche placed in a staircase display by the Roman Catholic Church; the other was a December holiday display that included a menorah, a Christmas tree, and a sign saluting liberty. The Court, without a majority opinion, invalidated the Nativity scene, but allowed the menorah. The key difference, at least for Justices Blackmun and O'Connor who cast the decisive votes, was that the Nativity scene was by itself and thus conveyed symbolic endorsement for Christianity; the menorah, in contrast, was accompanied by symbols of other religions and secular symbols.

We are in agreement with the three Justices—Stevens, Brennan, and Marshall—who would have found that both the Nativity scene and the menorah on government property violated the Establishment Clause.

Similarly, we believe that a cross—a quintessential Christian religious symbol—does not belong on government property. In *Capitol Square Review and Advisory Board v. Pinette*,[118] which we previously discussed, the Court in 1995 considered the Ku Klux Klan placing a large Latin cross in a public park across from the Ohio state capitol. The Supreme Court, without a majority opinion, found that the government's attempt to exclude the cross was unconstitutional discrimination against religious speech.

Likewise, in the most recent case, *American Legion v. American Humanist Association*,[119] also previously discussed, we strongly agree with Justice Ginsburg's dissent that understood the cross as a profoundly religious symbol that does not belong on government property. She observed: "An exclusively Christian symbol, the Latin cross is not emblematic of any other faith. The principal symbol of Christianity around the world should not loom over public thoroughfares, suggesting official recognition of that religion's paramountcy."[120]

Aid to Religious Institutions

Many Establishment Clause cases have involved the issue of government assistance to religion. Decisions in this area are numerous, but often difficult to reconcile. The Court inevitably is involved in line-drawing. Total government subsidy of churches or parochial schools undoubtedly would violate the Establishment Clause. Indeed, the famous statement of Thomas Jefferson concerning the need for a wall separating church and state and James Madison's Memorial and Remonstrance Against Religious Assessments were made in the context of opposing a state tax to aid the church.[121] But it also would be clearly unconstitutional if the government provided no public services—no police or fire protection, no sanitation services—to religious institutions. Such discrimination surely would violate equal protection and infringe on free exercise of religion.[122]

Therefore, the Court must draw a line between aid that is permissible and that which is forbidden. No bright-line test exists or likely ever will exist. Any aid provided to a religious institution or a parochial school frees resources that can be used to further its religious mission.[123] The dominant approach for the past half century has been to apply the test from *Lemon v. Kurtzman* and ask whether there is a secular purpose for the assistance, whether the aid has the effect of advancing religion, and whether the particular form of assistance causes excessive government entanglement with religion.[124] But not every case has used the *Lemon* test.

The decisions often seem difficult to reconcile. For example, the Court has upheld the government's providing buses to take children to and from parochial schools,[125] but not buses to take parochial school students on field trips.[126] The Court has permitted the government to pay for administering standardized tests in parochial schools,[127] but not for essay examinations assessing writing achievement.[128]

Although these distinctions often seem arbitrary, it is possible to identify several criteria that explain them. While not every case fits the pattern, in general the Court has been likely to uphold aid if three criteria are met. First, the aid must be available to all students enrolled in public and parochial schools; aid that is available only to parochial school students is sure to be invalidated. Second, the aid is more likely to be allowed if it is provided directly to the students than if it is provided to the schools. Third, the aid will be permitted if it is not actually used for religious instruction.

These criteria help explain the seemingly arbitrary distinctions previously described. For example, buses to take children to and from school are provided to students at all schools and are not involved in education itself, but buses for field trips to see cathedrals or religious icons might be seen differently. The content of state-prescribed standardized tests is secular, but teacher-written essay examinations might be on religious subjects.

These distinctions also help to explain why the government can provide—and must provide—police and fire protection and sanitation services to religious institutions, but that this does not mean that it must provide all forms of assistance that is given to private secular institutions. Police and fire protection and sanitation services are given to everyone in society. Providing these services to religious institutions serves a compelling secular purpose: without police protection, these places would be havens for crime; without fire protection, fires could spread to other structures; without sanitation services, public health would be endangered. That is why providing these services does not violate the Establishment Clause, while denying them would infringe free exercise of religion and equal protection. Yet it also is why these examples do not provide a basis for saying that other types of aid that are provided to secular private institutions must also be given to religions institutions.

But the law in this area is likely to change dramatically with a Court dominated by justices taking an accommodationist approach. The importance of the three theories of the Establishment Clause in the area of government aid to religious schools is reflected in *Mitchell v. Helms*.[129] *Mitchell*, which was decided in 2000, involved the provision of instructional equipment to parochial schools by Louisiana. Justice Thomas, writing for a plurality of four, said that the aid should be allowed because it is provided equally to all schools, religious and nonreligious.[130] He said that the key question is whether the government was participating in religious indoctrination. He wrote: "In distinguishing between indoctrination that is attributable to the State and indoctrination that is not, we have consistently turned to the principle of neutrality, upholding aid that is offered to a broad range of groups or persons without regard to their religion. If the religious, irreligious, and areligious are all alike eligible for governmental aid, no one would conclude that any indoctrination that any particular recipient conducts has been done at the behest of the government."[131] He rejected the argument that aid is impermissible because it might be diverted to religious use because any assistance could free funds that end up being used for religious purposes.

Justice Thomas emphatically rejected the view that the government cannot give aid that is actually used for religious education. He also sharply criticized the traditional doctrine preventing the government from giving aid to "pervasively sectarian" institutions. He said that this phrase was born of anti-Catholic bigotry and wrote that "hostility to aid to pervasively sectarian schools has a shameful pedigree that we do not hesitate to disavow."[132] He declared: "The inquiry into the recipient's religious views required by a focus on whether a school is pervasively sectarian is not only unnecessary but also offensive. It is well established, in numerous other contexts, that courts should refrain from trolling through a person's or institution's religious beliefs."[133] Taken literally, this would seem to require the government to give aid to parochial schools any time it is assisting secular private schools.

Justice O'Connor wrote an opinion concurring in the judgment, joined by Justice Breyer, in which she sharply disagreed with Justice Thomas's approach. Justice O'Connor said that equality never had been the sole measure of whether a government action violated the Establishment Clause. She wrote: "We have never held that a government-aid program passes constitutional muster solely because of the neutral criteria it employs as a basis for distributing aid. I also disagree with the plurality's conclusion that actual diversion of government aid to religious indoctrination is consistent with the Establishment Clause."[134] Justice O'Connor said that the test should be whether aid actually is used for religious instruction, in which case the Establishment Clause is violated.[135] Because she found no indication here that the aid was used for religious education in more than a negligible way, she found that the Louisiana program did not violate the First Amendment.

Justice Souter's dissenting opinion, joined by Justices Stevens and Ginsburg, urged the Court to adhere to its precedents and find that aid is impermissible when it is of a type, like instructional materials, that can be used for religious education. Justice Souter began by observing: "The establishment prohibition of government religious funding serves more than one end. It is meant to guarantee the right of individual conscience against compulsion, to protect the integrity of religion against the corrosion of secular support, and to preserve the unity of political society against the implied exclusion of the less favored and the antagonism of controversy over public support for religious causes."[136] He strongly disagreed with the plurality's view that equality is the sole test for the Establishment Clause and identified a number of factors that prior cases required to be considered in determining whether aid is impermissible.[137] Justice Souter powerfully concluded his dissent by stating: "In rejecting the principle of no aid to a school's religious mission the plurality is attacking the most fundamental assumption underlying the Establishment Clause, that government can in fact operate with neutrality in its relation to religion. I believe that it can, and so respectfully dissent."[138]

The rule that emerges from *Mitchell* is that the government cannot give aid if it is actually used for religious instruction. But the position taken by Justice Thomas, which was supported by four justices, likely can command a majority today: the government not only can give money that is used for religious instruction, but it must do so when it provides the assistance for private secular schools.

A strong indication of this is found in the Court's 2017 decision in *Trinity Lutheran Church of Columbia v. Comer*.[139] The Supreme Court, in a 7–2 decision, held that Missouri violated the rights of Trinity Lutheran under the Free Exercise Clause of the First Amendment by denying the church an otherwise available public benefit—aid to schools for a playground surface—on account of its religious status. Chief Justice Roberts wrote for the Court and said that Missouri was clearly discriminating against religious institutions in the receipt of this benefit and that therefore the state had to meet strict scrutiny under the Free Exercise Clause to justify the denial of the benefit. The Court declared: "Trinity Lutheran is a member of the community too, and the State's decision to exclude it for purposes of this public program must withstand the strictest scrutiny."[140]

The Court concluded that Missouri's denial of aid failed strict scrutiny. Providing this aid would not violate the Establishment Clause, and Missouri did not have a compelling interest in refusing to provide such aid.

The Court found that Missouri failed to meet strict scrutiny and Chief Justice Roberts concluded his opinion with the powerful statement: "But the exclusion of Trinity Lutheran from a public benefit for which it is otherwise qualified, solely because it is a church, is odious to our Constitution all the same, and cannot stand."[141]

Justice Sotomayor wrote a vehement dissent, joined by Justice Ginsburg, lamenting that this was the first time in history the Supreme Court ever found that the government was required to provide aid to a religious institution. She wrote: "This case is about nothing less than the relationship between religious institutions and the civil government—that is, between church and state. The Court today profoundly changes that relationship by holding, for the first time, that the Constitution requires the government to provide public funds directly to a church. Its decision slights both our precedents and our history, and its reasoning weakens this country's longstanding commitment to a separation of church and state beneficial to both."[142] She described the framers' desire to keep people from being taxed to support the religions of others.

Chief Justice Roberts addressed the limit to the reach of the Court's holding in footnote 3, where he wrote: "This case involves express discrimination based on religious identity with respect to playground resurfacing. We do not address religious uses of funding or other forms of discrimination."[143] Only three other Justices (Kennedy, Alito, and Kagan) joined this footnote.

It seems highly unlikely that *Trinity Lutheran* will be so limited; much more likely, it will be a basis for a broad requirement that the government *must* provide the same aid to religious institutions that it gives to secular ones. The majority in *Trinity Lutheran* sees discrimination against religious institutions as an infringement of free exercise of religion that must meet strict scrutiny. Chief Justice Roberts stated: "The Free Exercise Clause 'protect[s] religious observers against unequal treatment' and subjects to the strictest scrutiny laws that target the religious for 'special disabilities' based on their 'religious status.' "[144] The Court declared: "If the cases just described make one thing clear, it is that such a policy imposes a penalty on the free exercise of religion that triggers the most exacting scrutiny."[145] The Court thus explained "that the State's decision to exclude [Trinity Lutheran] for purposes of this public program must withstand the strictest scrutiny."[146] The Court concluded that Missouri's action was unconstitutional because it cannot survive strict scrutiny.

In coming to this conclusion, the Court had to distinguish, *Locke v. Davey*, the 2004 case in which the Court had to consider whether the government was constitutionally required to provide aid to support religion.[147] The Court, 7–2, rejected such a requirement. Chief

Justice William Rehnquist, obviously no liberal, wrote the opinion for the Court; only Justices Scalia and Thomas dissented.

Locke v. Davey arose from Washington's program of giving scholarships to students who qualify academically and financially and who attend college in the state. Students can attend any public or private college, including a religiously affiliated college, and may study whatever they choose. But there is one limit: students must not be pursuing a degree that is "devotional"; that is, the student cannot use the scholarship to study for training to become a minister. Washington justified this restriction based on a provision in its state constitution which provides that "no public money or property shall be appropriated for or applied to any religious worship, exercise or instruction, or the support of any religious establishment."[148]

Joshua Davey, a recipient of a Promise Scholarship, chose to attend Northwest College, a private Christian college affiliated with the Assemblies of God denomination. Davey sought to become a minister and had a double major in pastoral ministries and business management/administration. When Davey was informed that he could not receive the Promise Scholarship if he pursued training to become a minister, he refused the aid and filed a lawsuit challenging the restriction. Davey argued that Washington violated the Free Exercise Clause of the First Amendment by allowing students to receive scholarship assistance if they pursued secular, but not religious, studies.

The Court rejected that contention and ruled in favor of the State of Washington. At the outset, the Court emphasized that Washington could, if it wanted, allow its scholarships to be used by students studying to be clergy members. In *Witters v. Washington Dept. of Services for the Blind*,[149] the Supreme Court unanimously ruled in 1986 that it did not violate the Establishment Clause of the First Amendment for the government to permit students receiving scholarship assistance to study for the ministry.

In *Locke v. Davey*, the Court said that "there is room for play in the joints" between the Establishment Clause and the Free Exercise Clause.[150] The Court explained "there are some state actions permitted by the Establishment Clause but not required by the Free Exercise Clause."[151]

The Court explained that denying Davey scholarship money to study to be a minister does not interfere with his free exercise of religion in any way. He still can receive training to be a pastor, just without it being subsidized by the government. The Court stressed that many states historically have sought to limit use of their taxpayers' money to subsidize religious institutions.

Justice Scalia, in a dissent joined by Justice Thomas, argued that the denial of aid to Davey constituted hostility to religion that violated the Establishment Clause.[152] Chief Justice Rehnquist concluded his majority opinion by responding to and rejecting this argument:

> In short, we find neither in the history or text of Article I, § II, of the Washington Constitution, nor in the operation of the Promise Scholarship Program, anything that suggests animus toward religion. Given the historic and substantial state interest at issue, we therefore cannot conclude that the denial of funding for vocational religious instruction alone is inherently constitutionally suspect. Without a presumption of unconstitutionality, Davey's claim must fail. The State's interest in not funding the pursuit of devotional degrees is substantial and the exclusion of such funding places a relatively minor burden on Promise Scholars. If any room exists between the two Religion Clauses, it must be here.[153]

Locke v. Davey means that government at all levels can choose how it wants to spend taxpayers' money and the extent, if any, it wants to financially support religion. The Court recognized that the case posed an issue where there is some tension between the Establishment Clause and the Free Exercise Clause, but it concluded that it is a choice to be made by the political process and not the courts.

Under *Locke v. Davey*, it should have been permissible in *Trinity Lutheran* for Missouri to make the choice to subsidize secular private schools, but not religious ones. Missouri's decision, like Washington's, was to deny aid that could have been given without violating the Establishment Clause. The Court distinguished *Locke v. Davey* on two grounds.

First, the Court said: "Davey was not denied a scholarship because of who he was; he was denied a scholarship because of what he proposed to do—use the funds to prepare for the ministry. Here there is no question that Trinity Lutheran was denied a grant simply because of what it is—a church."[154]

Second, the Court said that *Locke v. Davey* involved aid for training a minister; whereas this case concerns assistance for playgrounds. Chief Justice Roberts wrote: "The Court in *Locke* also stated that Washington's choice was in keeping with the State's antiestablishment interest in not using taxpayer funds to pay for the training of clergy; in fact, the Court could 'think of few areas in which a State's antiestablishment interests come more into play.' . . . Here nothing of the sort can be said about a program to use recycled tires to resurface playgrounds."[155]

Both of these distinctions are very troubling and unpersuasive. As to the former, any time the government denies aid to parochial schools it is because of what they are: religious institutions. This would seem to make *any* denial of aid to religious schools unconstitutional when assistance is provided to secular private schools. Or, for that matter, it would make it unconstitutional to deny religious institutions any aid that is provided to secular institutions. Chief

Justice Roberts's distinction thus has dramatic implications: the government never would be able to deny financial assistance to religious institutions that is provided to secular ones.

For years, the government refused to provide faith-based institutions the assistance offered to secular institutions, whether for preschools or drug rehabilitation programs or other social services. Religious institutions could receive the aid, but they needed to create a secular arm to do so. The charitable choice movement has sought to allow faith-based institutions—churches, synagogues, mosques—to directly receive government assistance. There long has been debate over whether charitable choice is desirable and constitutional.[156]

The language in Chief Justice Roberts's opinion in *Trinity Lutheran* suggests that charitable choice may be a constitutional requirement. After all, the denial of aid always is because of what the institutions are: churches, synagogues, mosques.

Also, the distinction between what an institution is and what it does is inherently arbitrary. Religious institutions are different precisely because of what they do. Conversely, Joshua Davey was denied use of his scholarship because of what he was: a Christian who wanted to be ordained as a minister.

The Court's other distinction based on how the aid is used is equally troubling. As the Court often has observed, dollars are fungible. Aid provided for playgrounds frees up money for the parochial school to use for other purposes, including religious indoctrination. As Justice Sotomayor noted in her dissent: "The government may not directly fund religious exercise. Put in doctrinal terms, such funding violates the Establishment Clause because it impermissibly 'advanc[es] . . . religion.' Nowhere is this rule more clearly implicated than when funds flow directly from the public treasury to a house of worship. A house of worship exists to foster and further religious exercise. . . . When a government funds a house of worship, it underwrites this religious exercise."[157] Justice Sotomayor stressed that this is exactly the choice of the State of Washington in *Locke v. Davey* and of Missouri in denying religious schools aid for playgrounds: "Missouri has recognized the simple truth that, even absent an Establishment Clause violation, the transfer of public funds to houses of worship raises concerns that sit exactly between the Religion Clauses. To avoid those concerns, and only those concerns, it has prohibited such funding. In doing so, it made the same choice made by the earliest States centuries ago and many other States in the years since. The Constitution permits this choice."[158]

In other words, Chief Justice Roberts's attempts to distinguish *Locke v. Davey* are unpersuasive and have broad implications. Ultimately, the question in both cases was whether the government is constitutionally required to provide aid for religious instruction when it provides it for secular instruction. *Locke* says no; *Trinity Lutheran* says yes.

It appears that there now is a majority of the Court who will hold that the government *must* give aid to religious institutions when it provides it to secular private institutions.

As we complete this manuscript in spring 2020, there is a case pending before the Supreme Court which could lead to the government being obligated to provide benefits to religious institutions when they are given to private secular ones, *Espinoza v. Montana Department of Revenue.*[159] The Montana Supreme Court found that a state law that provided tax credits which benefited parochial schools violated the Montana Constitution. The Court granted review on the question of whether the exclusion of religion violates free exercise. We believe that this should be an easy case for the Court: the state supreme court declared unconstitutional a state law for violating the state constitution. A state should be able to limit its aid to religion and there should not be a constitutional obligation of the government to support religious institutions.

The Court's central argument is that it is unfair (and even "odious") to deny a church or other devotional institution an equal opportunity to compete for public funding merely because of its religious character (and particularly when such funding is purportedly for a secular purpose and the Court has ruled that government may voluntarily provide such benefits consistent with the Establishment Clause). However, as benign as this concern may seem on its surface, it is subject to a number of objections.

Most obviously, the Constitution itself mandates the disparate treatment of religious communities in regard to receiving public funding. As discussed earlier, the history of the Establishment Clause is in significant part about protecting against compelled funding of religious groups, which in turn makes it dubious to assert that government may provide even non-preferential financial assistance to churches.

Moreover, as also discussed earlier, when public funds are directed to churches or other worship institutions purportedly for secular purposes, they inevitably underwrite the devotional and proselytizing practices of those organizations. Or it becomes tempting to divert those funds to religious purposes, a concern that led the Court for many years to bar such aid if there was a risk of "excessive entanglement" between government and religion in policing the uses of such monies.[160]

As discussed earlier, the solution of the conservative wing of the Court—as illustrated by the plurality opinion in the *Helms* case—is simply to let such funding be used for religious purposes. And this seems to be where those justices intend the *Trinity Lutheran* decision to push the law, given the repeated assertions in the majority opinion about the unfairness of denying churches public funding while barely noting in a footnote (joined only by a plurality of justices) the significance of the fact that it was to be used in that case for purportedly secular purposes.[161] But a principle that would allow (or even worse, force) the government to directly fund the devotional practices and proselytization efforts of various religion sects, would surely alarm the generations of early Americans who came to understand free exercise and anti-establishment protections as being designed in significant part to protect against those very government actions.

Further, even if the Court were right to read the Religion Clauses as permitting the government to voluntarily provide funding to religious groups as part of a generally available funding program, it is quite another thing from a rights of conscience perspective to have judges *force* the government to do so. At least in the former situation, rights of conscience have had a chance to prevail in the resulting democratic decision to include religious institutions in government funding decisions. In such instances, any violations would presumably be confined to objecting minorities. But where judges compel funding through their own ideologically driven interpretations of the Religion Clauses, the infringement of conscience rights for objectors is potentially much more sweeping.

As we have argued, there are compelling reasons for treating religious institutions (as opposed to individuals) differently than secular organizations in regard to public funding—and particularly the use of compulsory taxation for such purposes. Many of the reasons that persuaded the founding generation that compelled taxpayer funding of churches and similar devotional or proselytizing institutions was "of a different ilk"[162] still apply today in a way that does not apply to such funding for secular institutions.

Most obviously, secular institutions do not use public money to underwrite devotional or proselytization activities, by which we mean the observance, celebration, or indoctrination of religious beliefs. But why, one may legitimately ask, is it a problem to compel funding to support such activities if a secular organization—and in particular an ideologically controversial one such as the National

Rifle Association—might use a public grant to celebrate and convince others of its views?

The short answer is that religious belief systems differ from secular belief systems in ways that make it incumbent on the government not to force members of the public to underwrite the former even if used to foster the latter. Freedom of religious belief occupies a special place in our historical and constitutional traditions. The framers of the First Amendment understood that there is a unique risk to the well-being of a political system to allow religious people to advocate policies that channel tax dollars to religious institutions. This was, perhaps, the central concern of the framers in deciding how the American republic should be different from the political systems they were previously familiar with. In the years leading up to the Constitution this question was front and center, including in the Virginia debates over disestablishment, which were central to the creation of the Constitution and Bill of Rights. Tax dollars are used for many things that individual taxpayers disagree with, but given their historical experience, the framers went out of their way to ensure that people could not fight over public moneys as a way of funding their churches and advancing their religious goals.

CONCLUSION

Soon before retiring from the Court, Justice Sandra Day O'Connor said: "By enforcing the [Religion] Clauses, we have kept religion a matter for the individual conscience, not for the prosecutor or bureaucrat. At a time when we see around the world the violent consequences of the assumption of religious authority by government, Americans may count themselves fortunate: Our regard for constitutional boundaries has protected us from similar travails, while allowing private religious exercise to flourish. . . . Those who would renegotiate the boundaries between church and state must therefore answer a difficult question: Why would we trade a system that has served us so well for one that has served others so poorly?"[163]

Why indeed? It is why we believe that a separationist approach is the best way of interpreting the Establishment Clause and it is why we lament the direction of the current Court. Advocates for the greater recognition of religion in government action often say they feel disrespected or oppressed when people work to ensure that the government remain secular. We think such expressions of harm are not well justified. It is not disrespectful to the faithful who have witnessed an end to their prayers said in schools and in government functions, or an end to public monies to support their religious endeavors (but not those of many other sects), to say that we have decided to be even more faithful to the framers' goal of a truly secular republic. When the country has made progress in black civil rights, the status of women in society, or the circumstances of the LGBTQ community, it has often required an end to the privileged status of historically advantaged groups. Disestablishing the privileged status of some has often created the conditions for a new normal that is more inclusive. Our separationist approach is consistent with advancing more inclusive vision of religious liberty in our constitutional system.

CHAPTER FOUR

The Free Exercise of Religion

*Guarding against Religious Animus but Defending Neutral
Laws of General Applicability*

Congress shall make no law . . . prohibiting the free exercise [of
religion] . . .

WHEN WE THINK about a person engaging in a religious practice it
is easy to conjure up images of people attending worship services,
participating in scripture study or prayer groups, following dietary
restrictions, engaging in private devotions, or following religious
rituals at home. Very few contemporary debates about the scope
of religious liberty involve efforts by the government to shut down
religious services, ban prayer groups, or prohibit the celebration of
religious holidays with family and friends.

Instead, the most contentious issues revolve around claims that
people's free exercise of religion includes not only the freedom to associate with a religion of their choice and engage in formal acts of worship but also the freedom to resist otherwise general laws when those
laws require them to act in ways that are inconsistent with their faith.

These include claims by some parents that they have a right to deny their children vaccinations or restrict their access to medical care when their religious convictions demand instead that they rely on the healing power of prayer. Court clerks whose religion defines a marriage as a union of a man and woman have asserted a right to refuse marriage licenses to same-sex couples, and religious business owners seek exemptions from anti-discrimination laws so that they might refuse services in support of same-sex weddings. Religious employers demand a right to deny insurance coverage to employees for contraception when non-religious employers are legally required to cover contraception. Pharmacists want the right to not fill prescriptions for medical procedures that are inconsistent with their beliefs.[1]

What underlies the debate is the profound question of how to reconcile the practices and beliefs of a diverse set of religious practitioners with the secular authority of the American people to advance their interests and values. Ordinary politics occurs within a cauldron of competing interests and values, with results that almost never satisfy everyone and are frequently considered inconsistent with the strongly held beliefs of large numbers of people. In diverse, representative societies, we treat disagreeable outcomes as an inevitable feature of politics, and we urge those whose interests or values are undermined or burdened to go back into the political area and try harder to convince their fellow citizens or representatives to care more about their issues.

But should that assumption be different when the interests or values being burdened arise from convictions of religious faith and practice? Does the Constitution obligate government to be more accommodating of religious perspectives than secular ones, for example, by mandating exemptions to social duties that impose burdens on religious practitioners even if they also impose burdens on non-religious people who hold similar views? How much should a secular society accommodate the interests and perspectives of a religiously diverse people?

In this chapter we examine the meaning of the Free Exercise Clause. We begin by describing competing theories of what this constitutional provision requires of government. We then defend our view that the Free Exercise Clause prohibits government action that is motivated by animus toward particular religions or religious practitioners or that targets religious beliefs, institutions, and practices, but it does not provide a basis for exceptions from neutral laws of general applicability even if such laws impose burdens or inconveniences on religious people. We conclude this chapter by applying this vision to some of the most important contemporary issues concerning the Free Exercise Clause, including whether religious employers or providers have a right to withhold health benefits that violate their religious convictions, and whether religious business owners should be granted the religious liberty to deny services to same-sex couples.

COMPETING THEORIES OF THE FREE EXERCISE CLAUSE

There are three major competing approaches to the Free Exercise Clause. The first theory represents the Court's first foray into these disputes in the late 19th century and has few adherents among today's judges and commentators since it has been seen as offering too narrow an understanding of the clause. The other two are supported by a vast body of scholarly literature and by a wide range of judges and law professors. Disagreements about these competing theories persist within the judiciary and within the political system more broadly, with Congress and state legislatures weighing in on the controversies.

Protecting Religious Belief but Not Conduct

The Supreme Court's first major decision on the Free Exercise Clause was *Reynolds v. United States* (1879) and involved controversies surrounding the Mormon (Latter Day Saints) practice of polygamy.[2] Mormons had begun settling in the Utah territories in the 1840s, even before Mexico ceded the territory to the United States at the end of the Mexican-American War. During much of the 1850s the territory enjoyed relative autonomy from federal control, under the leadership of Brigham Young. But relations with the federal government became strained when reports reached Washington that Mormon leaders had publicly sanctioned the practice of polygamy. In 1857, President James Buchanan removed Brigham Young, who had 20 wives, from his position as governor of the territory, and sent US troops to Utah to establish federal authority. In 1862, Congress passed the Morrill Anti-Bigamy Act, which banned bigamy in federal territories such as Utah.[3]

George Reynolds was Brigham Young's secretary. After marrying a woman while still married to his previous wife, he was charged with violating the Morrill Act. Reynolds argued that the law violated the Free Exercise Clause, because his religion required him to marry multiple women.

In a unanimous decision, the Supreme Court upheld Reynold's conviction and Congress's power to prohibit polygamy. Chief Justice Waite's opinion elaborated a distinction that for a while would prove helpful in adjudicating free exercise cases. He explained that the First Amendment deprived Congress "of all legislative power over mere opinion" but left the legislature "free to reach actions which were in violation of social duties or subversive of good order." Although laws "cannot interfere with mere religious belief and opinion, they may with practices. Suppose one believed that human sacrifices were a necessary part of religious worship, would it be seriously contended that the civil government under which he lived could not interfere to prevent a sacrifice?" He continued:

> As a law of the organization of society under the exclusive dominion of the United States, it is provided that plural marriages shall not be allowed. Can a man excuse his practices to the contrary because of his religious belief? To permit this would be to make the professed doctrines of religious belief superior to the law of the land, and in effect permit every citizen to become a law unto himself. Government could exist only in name under such circumstances.[4]

In other words, while the Free Exercise Clause prohibited the federal government from criminalizing a person's attachment to a set of religious beliefs, it did not bar the regulation of conduct, especially when such conduct was inconsistent with broader "social duties" or otherwise "subversive of good order." It was fine to believe what you want, but the First Amendment did not exempt a religious practitioner from having to obey the same rules that regulate everyone else's behavior, even if those rules infringed on religious precepts. If a religious belief allowed a person to disregard otherwise general laws, then it would "permit every citizen to become a law unto himself" and would destroy the very foundations of government.

The "belief versus conduct" dichotomy was an easy way to frame the scope of the protection for free exercise, but there were obvious problems with that simple formulation. Most important, the Constitution protects the "exercise" of religion, and not just the freedom to hold certain beliefs. It would be a hollow right if individuals were allowed to proclaim their belief in the precepts of Judaism (for example) but were prohibited by law to gather in synagogues, wear religious garb, or follow Judaism's dietary restrictions. Moreover, by limiting the protection of free exercise to religious beliefs, *Reynolds* left very little content to this clause in the First Amendment. Rarely will government outlaw beliefs; laws regulate conduct, not views.

The *Reynolds* Court said Congress was deprived "of all legislative power over mere opinion" but "free to reach actions which were in violation of social duties or subversive of good order." This was explicit that religious belief could not exempt a person from general social obligations, but it did not make clear enough that government could not target religious practitioners by prohibiting the conduct associated with the details of their religious worship. This way of putting the point would have been more consistent with some of the language used by those of the founding generation when explaining their views on the Free Exercise Clause. For example, Thomas Jefferson declared that while religion was to be protected in its "doctrines, discipline, or exercises," it had no right to be excluded from "social duties."[5]

This move from mere belief to other core aspects of religious practice was made a bit clearer 11 years later. At issue in *Davis v. Beason* (1890) was an edict by the territory of Idaho that limited voting rights to men who swore an oath that they did not practice polygamy or belong to an organization that encourages polygamy. Justice Field wrote for a unanimous Court upholding the law on the grounds that bigamy and polygamy are crimes "by the laws of all civilized and Christian countries. . . . To call their advocacy a tenet of religion is to offend the common sense of mankind. If they are crimes, then to teach, advise, and counsel their practice is to aid in their commission." More generally, he announced that the First Amendment

> was intended to allow every one under the jurisdiction of the
> United States to entertain such notions respecting his relations
> to his Maker and the duties they impose as may be approved by

his judgment and conscience, and to exhibit his sentiments in such form of worship as he may think proper, not injurious to the equal rights of others, and to prohibit legislation for the support of any religious tenets, or the modes of worship of any sect. The oppressive measures adopted, and the cruelties and punishments inflicted, by the governments of Europe for many ages, to compel parties to conform, in their religious beliefs and modes of worship, to the views of the most numerous sect, and the folly of attempting in that way to control the mental operations of persons, and enforce an outward conformity to a prescribed standard, led to the adoption of the amendment in question. It was never intended or supposed that the amendment could be invoked as a protection against legislation for the punishments of acts inimical to the peace, good order, and morals of society.

The Court said that there have been sects that have advocated "promiscuous intercourse of the sexes" and even "human sacrifices," but "no heed" should be "given to the pretense that, as religious beliefs, their supporters could be protected in their exercise" by the Constitution. To rule otherwise "would be to make the professed doctrines of religious belief superior to the law of the land, and in effect to permit every citizen to become a law unto himself. Government could exist only in name under such circumstances. . . . Crime is not the less odious because sanctioned by what any particular sect may designate as religion."[6]

This general approach persisted through the mid-20th century. For example, in *Prince v. Massachusetts* (1944) the Court upheld a state law making it a crime for children to sell merchandise in public places as applied to a child who was distributing religious literature with her guardian. The Court rejected a claim that the free exercise of religion was violated by the law. The majority emphasized the state's interest in "the healthy, well-rounded growth of young

people" and "the crippling effects of child employment."[7] Most state
courts followed this same approach. When the New York Court of
Appeals was asked to respect the rights of a man who sought to heal
a sick child by prayer rather than by seeking traditional medical
assistance, the judges refused, explaining that "full and free enjoyment of religious profession and worship is guarantied but acts which
are not worship are not."[8]

Strict Scrutiny of Laws Burdening Religious Freedom

This approach was not significantly challenged until the early 1960s.
At issue in *Braunfeld v. Brown* (1961) was whether Pennsylvania's
Sunday Closing Law—requiring commercial establishments to cease
business on Sunday—violated the free exercise rights of Orthodox
Jews. The claim was that, as a result of this law, Christians and others
who were "Sunday sabbatarians" were free to engage in business
practices six days a week, but Orthodox Jews and other "non-Sunday
sabbatarians" would only be able to engage in commercial activities
five days a week (Sunday plus the day of their Sabbath), thus putting
them in an unequal position with respect to the right "to earn a
livelihood."

The plurality opinion was written by Chief Justice Warren, and
in most of the opinion he reiterated the position the Court had embraced since *Reynolds*. "Legislative power over mere opinion is forbidden, but it may reach people's actions when they are found to be
in violation of important social duties or subversive of the good order,
even when the actions are demanded by one's religion." Warren argued that to "strike down . . . legislation which imposes only an indirect burden on the exercise of religion . . . would radically restrict
the operating latitude of the legislature. Statutes which tax income
and limit the amount which may be deducted for religious contri-
butions impose an indirect economic burden on the observance of

the religion of the citizen whose religion requires him to donate a greater amount to his church; statutes which require the courts to be closed on Saturday and Sunday impose a similar indirect burden on the observance of the religion of the trial lawyer whose religion requires him to rest on a weekday."

However, in an addition to the traditional "protect beliefs but not conduct" approach, Warren suggested that the important constitutional question centered on whether the burdensome government regulation had a secular purpose or was designed to impede an otherwise unobjectionable religious practice. "If the purpose or effect of a law is to impede the observance of one or all religions or is to discriminate invidiously between religions, that law is constitutionally invalid even though the burden may be characterized as being only indirect. But if the State regulates conduct by enacting a general law within its power, the purpose and effect of which is to advance the State's secular goals, the statute is valid despite its indirect burden on religious observances *unless the State may accomplish its purpose by means which do not impose such a burden.*"

This last phrase pointed the way to a new approach: a secular law may be invalid if it could accomplish its goals without indirectly burdening religious practitioners. In the language of constitutional law, Warren was suggesting a "least restrictive means" test, meaning that the legislature was obligated to promote its secular goals in a manner that was "least restrictive" of religious freedom. Although not made explicit in Warren's opinion, this approach is typically referred to in constitutional doctrine as applying "strict scrutiny" to certain categories of laws—in this case, laws that burden religious practitioners either directly or indirectly. If there is such a burden it is not enough that the legislative purpose be legitimate; it is also necessary for there to be no other way to accomplish the goal.

Justice Brennan, in his dissenting opinion, was more explicit about what he considered the appropriate test for these kinds of cases. He argued that the Court should take greater pains to weigh the government's interest against the burden imposed on religious practice. He felt that the Free Exercise Clause prohibited government from advancing a trivial interest at the expense of religious freedom. He noted that the law's "effect is that appellants may not simultaneously practice their religion and their trade, without being hampered by a substantial competitive disadvantage" and asked "What, then, is the compelling government interest which impels Pennsylvania to impede appellants' freedom of worship? . . . It is not the desire to stamp out a practice deeply abhorred by society, such as polygamy, as in *Reynolds*, [nor] is it the State's traditional protection of children, as in *Prince*. . . . It is not even the interest in seeing that everyone rests one day a week, for appellants' religion requires that they take such a rest. It is the mere convenience of having everyone rest on the same day."[9]

This language captures in full the typical "strict scrutiny/compelling state interest/least restrictive means" test that is normally associated with the protection of fundamental liberties in the modern era of Supreme Court decision making. And it would not take long for the Court to formally adopt this approach.

Two years after *Braunfeld*, the Court heard what appeared to be a very similar case but came to a very different conclusion, and in so doing, it created a new test for evaluating free exercise claims that would shape the Court's approach for the next 27 years.

In *Sherbert v. Verner* (1963), a Seventh-day Adventist, discharged by her employer "because she would not work on Saturday, the Sabbath Day of her faith," was denied unemployment compensation by South Carolina on the ground that she refused to accept "suitable work," which in her case meant a job that required her to work on her Sabbath.

Brennan, who dissented in *Braunfeld*, wrote the majority opinion for the Court reversing the state's determination. For the first time, the Court held that a general law that imposed an indirect burden on religious practice had to be subjected to "strict scrutiny." Brennan argued that the "burden on the free exercise of appellant's religion" must be justified, not by ordinary justifications, but by a truly "compelling state interest." In this case the Court held that the justification for the burden on Verner was simply not compelling enough. "Appellees suggest no more than a possibility that the filing of fraudulent claims by unscrupulous claimants feigning religious objections to Saturday work [might] dilute the unemployment compensation fund [but] there is no proof whatever to warrant such fears of malingering or deceit [and] it is highly doubtful whether such evidence would be sufficient to warrant a substantial infringement of religious liberties. For [it] would plainly be incumbent upon the appellees to demonstrate that no alternative forms of regulation would combat such abuses without infringing First Amendment rights."

Justice Douglas wrote a concurring opinion in which he expressed the view that "the interference here is as plain as it is in Soviet Russia, where a churchgoer is given a second-class citizenship, resulting in harm though perhaps not in measurable damages." Justices Harlan and White dissented, arguing that the state was merely treating Verner like any other claimant, and that while the state legislature may choose to accommodate religious practitioners, there was no constitutional requirement that it do so.[10]

Although this was a dramatic departure from the Court's traditional jurisprudence, the justices applied it in only two limited settings over the next 30 years: cases like *Sherbert* involving the denial of benefits to those who quit their jobs for religious reasons[11] and the application of a compulsory school law to the Amish. In all other instances, the Supreme Court rejected the Free Exercise Clause claims and efforts to assert religious exemptions from general laws.

Wisconsin v. Yoder (1972) involved members of the Amish Church who declined to send their children to schools after they had completed the eighth grade. They were convicted for violating a law compelling parents to send their kids to school up to the age of 16 and fined $5 each. They believed that by sending their children to any of the publicly or privately run high schools, they would endanger their own salvation and that of their children, since their faith placed a premium on learning-through-doing, manual labor, and community welfare, and objected to values like competitiveness and self-distinction which they believed were prevalent in high schools. The state stipulated that respondents' religious beliefs were sincere.

The Court, in an opinion by Chief Justice Burger, overturned their conviction. Burger placed great emphasis on the fact that the Amish's objections to compulsory non-elementary education were based on deeply held and verifiable religious convictions and not "subjective," "secular," "philosophical," or "personal" evaluations and preferences, which, Burger argued, would not be covered by the Free Exercise Clause. "It cannot be overemphasized that we are not dealing with a way of life and mode of education by a group claiming to have recently discovered some 'progressive' or more enlightened process for rearing children for modern life." Burger also thought it relevant that the Amish community had a record of being "productive and very law-abiding"; he thought it worth adding that they even "reject public welfare."

Once he established that the Amish exhibited a respectable and traditional way of life and were not a bunch of wild, irresponsible hippies, he then noted that "the impact of the compulsory-attendance law on respondents' practice of the Amish religion is not only severe, but inescapable, for the Wisconsin law affirmatively compels them, under threat of criminal sanctions, to perform acts undeniably at odds with fundamental tenets of their religious faith." As such, the law posed "a very real threat of undermining the Amish community and religious practices." The Court also stressed that application of the Wisconsin compulsory schooling law to the Amish would infringe the constitutional right of parents to control the upbringing of their children.

Justices White, Brennan, and Stewart concurred in the outcome but wrote separately to emphasize that "the sincerity of the Amish religious policy here is uncontested, the potential adverse impact of the state requirement is great and the State's valid interest in education has already been largely satisfied by the eight years the children have already spent in school."

Justice Douglas's partial dissent stressed that the Court needed to be more solicitous to the possibility that some Amish children might want additional public education in case they chose to move away from the community. "If a parent keeps his child out of school beyond the grade school, then the child will be forever barred from entry into the new and amazing world of diversity that we have today." By giving the child the opportunity to be educated the state was empowering the child to choose to remain in the Amish community or to make another choice; privileging the Amish community's strategy for ensuring ongoing membership over the state's interest in educating the young elevates religious interests over secular state interests. "It is the student's judgment, not his parents', that is essential if we are to give full meaning to what we have said about the Bill of Rights and the right of students to be masters of their own destiny. If he is harnessed to the Amish way of life by those in authority over him and if his education is truncated, his entire life may be stunted and deformed."[12]

The opinion in *Yoder* highlights a number of pitfalls with the "strict scrutiny" approach to burdens on religious practitioners. The emphasis in Chief Justice Burger's opinion on the positive, law-abiding qualities of the Amish community implies that special accommodations for religious practitioners may be available only to religious sects that are favored by judges on religious or ideological grounds. This is in direct contradiction to the Constitution's clear concern that there be no special religious favorites of the government.[13] Those comments in the opinion were so odd that they led Justice Douglas in dissent to clarify that "the emphasis of the Court on the 'law and order' record of this Amish group of people is quite irrelevant. A religion is a religion irrespective of what the misdemeanor or felony records of its members might be. I am not at all sure how the Catholics, Episcopalians, the Baptists, Jehovah's Witnesses, the Unitarians, and my own Presbyterians would make out if we were subjected to such a test."[14]

It is also not obvious that denying education to children under 16 is harmless, or that the state should not be free to make a decision about whether it is in the public interest to require education of children up through grade 8 or 10 or 12. The Court emphasized that lack of "two . . . additional years of compulsory education will not impair the physical or mental health of the child . . . or in any other way materially detract from the welfare of society." But this discounts the state's asserted interest in ensuring that children are properly educated so that they are in a position to make important decisions about their lives and futures.[15]

The Court's *Yoder* opinion had the potential of embroiling the justices in very complicated and controversial assessments of the value of certain religious practices and the importance of various government interests. However, even while formally applying the new "strict scrutiny" standard, the Court for the next 18 years upheld general laws against challenges from religious practitioners.

For example, 10 years after *Yoder*, in *United States v. Lee* (1982), the Court held that the Free Exercise Clause does not require an exemption for members of the Old Order Amish from payment of social security taxes even though the Court accepted their contention "that both payment and receipt of social security benefits is forbidden by the Amish faith." In his opinion for the Court, Chief Justice Burger explained that "the state may justify a limitation on religious liberty by showing that it is essential to accomplish an overriding governmental interest," and the justices concluded that "mandatory participation is indispensable to the fiscal vitality of the social security system." The Court reiterated that "[in order to] maintain an organized society that guarantees religious freedom to a great variety of faiths requires that some religious practices yield to the common good" and added the obvious point that "[the] tax system could not function if denominations were allowed to challenge the tax system because tax payments were spent in a manner that violates their religious belief." Justice Stevens wrote separately in order to emphasize an additional consideration, namely, "the overriding interest in keeping the government—whether the legislature or the courts—out of the business of evaluating the relative merits of differing religious claims" since "the risk that governmental approval of some and disapproval of others will be perceived as favoring one religion over another is an important risk the Establishment Clause was designed to preclude."[16]

In other cases the Court ruled that the Free Exercise Clause was not violated when

- the IRS denied tax exempt status to private schools that practice racial discrimination on the basis of sincerely held religious beliefs [*Bob Jones University v. United States* (1983)];[17]
- an Orthodox Jewish psychologist who worked for the Air Force was required to abide by its uniform dress requirement even though that meant he could not wear a yarmulke while on duty at a military hospital [*Goldman v. Weinberger* (1986)];[18]
- a prison's enforcement of work regulations prevented Muslim prisoners from attending a weekly religious service important to their faith [*O'Lone v. Estate of Shabazz* (1987)];[19] and

- the government utilized social security numbers as a condition for a family's receipt of AFDC and Food Stamps despite claims from a Native American family that their use supported a technology that was "robbing the spirit of man" [*Bowen v. Roy* (1986)].[20]

If *Yoder* highlights some of the problems associated with applying strict scrutiny to government action that incidentally burdens religious practitioners, *Lyng v. Northwest Indian Cemetery Protective Association* (1988) highlights the serious impact that unchecked government action can have on the free exercise of religion. In that case the Court held that the federal government's road construction and timber harvesting in a national forest did not violate the free exercise rights of Native American tribes even though these activities would irreparably damage "sacred areas which are an integral and necessary part of [their] belief systems" and "virtually destroy the Indians' ability to practice their religion."

Citing language in *Bowen v. Roy*, Justice O'Connor explained that the "Free Exercise Clause affords an individual protection from certain forms of governmental compulsion; it does not afford an individual a right to dictate the conduct of the Government's internal procedures." In an adjustment from the *Sherbert/Yoder* approach, the Court held that rules evaluating government action should be different depending on whether the government was directly prohibiting religious practice or was instead acting under general rules that just happen to impose indirect (non-targeted or intentional) burdens on religious practitioners. Rather than require each action to be justified by a compelling interest and an analysis of least restrictive alternatives, the Court ruled that there should be no requirement for a "compelling justification" when evaluating the "incidental effects of government programs, which may make it more difficult to practice certain religions but which have no tendency to coerce individuals into acting contrary to their religious beliefs."

The majority noted that "the crucial word in the constitutional text is 'prohibit,'" and that "the Free Exercise Clause is written in terms of what the government cannot do to the individual, not in terms of what the individual can exact from the government."

Justice O'Connor declared that

> government simply could not operate if it were required to satisfy every citizen's religious needs and desires. A broad range of government activities—from social welfare programs to foreign aid to conservation projects—will always be considered essential to the spiritual wellbeing of some citizens, often on the basis of sincerely held religious beliefs. Others will find the very same activities deeply offensive, and perhaps incompatible with their own search for spiritual fulfillment and with the tenets of their religion. The First Amendment must apply to all citizens alike, and it can give to none of them a veto over public programs that do not prohibit the free exercise of religion.

She also argued that the position of the dissenters would put the Court in the position of weighing the value of every religious belief against the government's interest in particular programs. The dissent "proposes a legal test under which it would decide which public lands are 'central' or 'indispensable' to which religions, and by implication which are 'dispensable' or 'peripheral,' and would then decide which government programs are 'compelling' enough to justify 'infringement of those practices.' We would accordingly be required to weigh the value of every religious belief and practice that is said to be threatened by any government program. . . . In other words, the dissent's approach would require us to rule that some religious adherents misunderstand their own religious beliefs. We think such an approach cannot be squared with the Constitution."

Brennan, Marshall, and Blackmun dissented, pointing out the unprecedented—in fact, totally devastating—effect that this government action would have on religious practice and contrasting it with the government's interest in lumber profits. "Today's ruling sacrifices a religion at least as old as the Nation itself, along with the spiritual well-being of its 5,000 adherents, so that the Forest Service can build a six-mile segment of road that two lower courts found had only the most marginal and speculative utility." The dissenters argued that religious practitioners challenging a government action under the Free Exercise Clause should be required to show that a government program would substantially threaten religious practice. Once shown, the government should be required to articulate a compelling state interest sufficient to justify the infringement of that practice. As for the majority's distinction between laws that directly prohibit religious practices versus those that impose indirect burdens, the dissenters argued that "religious freedom is threatened no less by governmental action that makes the practice of one's chosen faith impossible than by governmental programs that pressure one to engage in conduct inconsistent with religious beliefs."[21]

Those in favor of the strict scrutiny approach had in mind circumstances like the one presented in *Lyng*, where a relatively unimportant public interest was sufficient to seriously interfere with the ability of religious minorities to practice their faith. To the dissenters, it is no consolation to tell the religious practitioners to seek accommodation within the political process, because it is precisely their status as relatively powerless members of a less mainstream religion that puts them in a vulnerable position in the first place and that makes judicial protection of their interests well justified.[22] Because more mainstream or powerful religions were less likely to find themselves in these vulnerable positions, special judicial protection for more vulnerable practitioners helped ensure greater equality of protection all around for the free exercise of religion. On this view, strict scrutiny gave religious outliers the same kinds of immunity against burdensome government action that mainstream practitioners experienced all the time.

Still, for the period between 1963 and 1988, when the Court was acting under a "strict scrutiny" approach to the Free Exercise Clause, the justices rarely found violations. After 25 years of experimenting with requirements to find compelling state interests and least restrictive alternatives, a majority on the Court was ready to move on to a new theory.

Employment Division v. Smith *and No Exemptions from Neutral Laws of General Applicability*

In 1990, the majority on the Court abandoned applying strict scrutiny to any government action that directly or indirectly prohibited or burdened religious practitioners. *Employment Division v. Smith* (1990) arose after Native Americans were fired from their jobs at a drug rehabilitation clinic because it was discovered that they had ingested peyote as part of a sacrament during a ceremony at the Native American Church. The state of Oregon turned them down for unemployment benefits on the basis of a policy that withholds benefits from people who were fired as a result of "misconduct," with the misconduct in this case involving action that violated the state's criminal anti-drug statutes. They challenged the application of this state policy in their case on the ground that it amounted to an infringement of their freedom of religion, since the basis upon which the state denied them unemployment compensation was related to their religious practice—just as had been the case years earlier in *Sherbert*.

In an opinion by Justice Scalia, the Court upheld the denial of unemployment compensation. Scalia reasoned that "if a State has prohibited through its criminal laws certain kinds of religiously

motivated conduct without violating the First Amendment"—
for example, prohibiting the use of peyote even during religious
rituals—"it certainly follows that it may impose the lesser burden
of denying unemployment compensation benefits to persons who
engage in that conduct."

By this point the justices had tried various theories governing a
variety of free exercise activities, including the holding of religious
beliefs, the activities surrounding formal acts of worship, and related
conduct that was religiously inspired. Justice Scalia's approach was
to place these activities into different categories for purposes of constitutional analysis:

> [The] free exercise of religion means, first and foremost, the
> right to believe and profess whatever religious doctrine one de-
> sires. . . . But the "exercise of religion" often involves not only
> belief and profession but the performance of (or abstention from)
> physical acts: assembling with others for a worship service, par-
> ticipating in sacramental use of bread and wine, proselytizing,
> abstaining from certain foods or certain modes of transportation.
> It would be true, we think (though no case of ours has involved
> this point), that a state would be "prohibiting the free exercise [of
> religion]" if it sought to ban such acts or abstentions only when
> they are engaged in for religious reasons, or only because of the
> religious belief that they display. It would doubtless be uncon-
> stitutional, for example, to ban the casting of "statues that are
> to be used for worship purposes," or to prohibit bowing down
> before a golden calf.

The main point of the majority's discussion, however, was to distinguish these examples from those cases when the government prohibition was directed at conduct that was not specifically religious in
nature, as was the case with anti-drug laws, and where the regulation

was not based on animus toward religion. "We have never held that an individual's religious beliefs excuse him for compliance with an otherwise valid law prohibiting conduct that the State is free to regulate. . . . [In] *Prince*, we held that a mother could be prosecuted under the child labor laws for using her children to dispense literature in the streets, her religious motivation notwithstanding." Scalia suggested that the only time the Court had barred the application of neutral, general laws to religiously motivated action had been when the Free Exercise Clause acted in conjunction with other rights, such as the right of parents to educate their children as they see fit, as in the case of the Amish and compulsory education laws.

The majority's main concern with the application of strict scrutiny to neutral laws of general applicability is that it would substitute the assumption that everyone was equal under the law to an obligation to provide a wide range of ad hoc religious exemptions to a wide range of laws and regulations:

> The rule respondents favor would open the prospect of constitutionally required religious exemptions from civic obligations of almost every conceivable kind—ranging from compulsory military service, to the payment of taxes, to health and safety regulation such as manslaughter and child neglect laws, compulsory vaccination laws, drug laws, and traffic laws, to social welfare legislation such as minimum wage laws, child labor laws, animal cruelty laws, environmental protection laws, and laws providing for equality of opportunity for the races. The First Amendment's protection of religious liberty does not require this.

All such laws had good reasons behind them, but if in every circumstance where a religious practitioner felt burdened the government was required to come up with a "compelling" interest in the law then "many laws would not meet the test." In fact, "precisely because we value and protect [] religious divergence, we cannot afford the luxury of deeming *presumptively invalid*, as applied to the religious objector, every regulation of conduct that does not protect an interest of the highest order."

The majority argued that the only way to make such an approach manageable would be to limit strict scrutiny to those circumstances where the burden on religion was central rather than merely incidental. However, in their view, "it is no more appropriate for judges to determine the 'centrality' of religious beliefs before applying a 'compelling interest' test in the free exercise field than it would be for them to determine the 'importance' of ideas before applying the 'compelling interest' test in the free speech field. What principle of law or logic can be brought to bear to contradict a believer's assertion that a particular act is 'central' to his personal faith?"

Scalia summarized his concerns in his conclusion: "A number of States have made an exception to their drug laws for sacramental peyote use. But to say that a nondiscriminatory religious-practice exemption is permitted, or even that it is desirable, is not to say that it is constitutionally required, and that the appropriate occasions for its creation can be discerned by the courts." For Justice Scalia and the majority, it should be left to the political process, not to the courts, to create exemptions to general laws. A state certainly could provide Native Americans an exception from peyote laws, but it is not for the judiciary to do so in enforcing free exercise of religion. Justice Scalia stated: "It may fairly be said that leaving accommodation to the political process will place at a relative disadvantage those religious practices that are not widely engaged in; but that unavoidable consequence of democratic government must be preferred to a system in which each conscience is a law unto itself or in which judges weigh the social importance of all laws against the centrality of all religious beliefs."

O'Connor wrote a concurring opinion, part of which was joined by Brennan, Marshall, and Blackmun, disagreeing with the abandonment of the strict scrutiny approach in cases such as this. "The Court [today] interprets the [Free Exercise] Clause to permit the government to prohibit, without justification, conduct mandated by an individual's religious beliefs, so long as that prohibition is generally applicable." In her view, this was too narrow a reading of the protections offered by the Constitution, since in essence the Court was only offering constitutional protection when government was explicitly motivated by a desire to oppress a particular religious minority, and "if the First Amendment is to have any vitality, it ought not be construed to cover only the extreme and hypothetical situation in which a State directly targets a religious practice." It was no consolation to say that, in all other cases, religious practitioners had to appeal to the political process, since "the First Amendment was enacted precisely to protect the rights of those whose religious practices are not shared by the majority and may be viewed with hostility."

In a part of her opinion that was not joined by the liberals, O'Connor applied the *Sherbert* test to the facts in this case and upheld the denial of unemployment compensation. While she considered it a close call, she was of the opinion that the uniform application of Oregon's drug laws was essential to accomplishing the state's compelling interest.

Blackmun, Brennan, and Marshall dissented. They argued that the Court should weigh the state's interest in refusing to grant an exemption to Native Americans against the effect that the uniform application of the law would have on the Native Americans' free exercise. They noted, "Without peyote, they could not enact the essential ritual of their religion." By contrast, the State presented no evidence at all that the religious use of peyote has ever harmed anyone, and there is no evidence that there is an illegal traffic in peyote. According to the dissenters, these two points distinguish the claim of Native Americans from the claims of religions such as the Ethiopian Zion Coptic, which teaches that marijuana should be smoked continually all day. While the government had a compelling interest to pass drug laws, it did not have a compelling interest to apply those laws to the particular circumstances of these religious practitioners.[23]

Smith brought an end to the Court's 27-year experiment in extending greater protections to religious practitioners even when government action did not seem motivated by animus. Although the majority might have felt relief with not having to weigh or assess religious interests versus government interests, not everyone was happy with the Court's decision to set aside strict scrutiny in these cases. Congress responded to *Smith* by passing the Religious Freedom Restoration Act, often referred to as "RFRA." The act declared that its purpose was "to restore the compelling interest test as set forth in Sherbert v. Verner and Wisconsin v. Yoder, and to guarantee its application in all cases where free exercise of religion is substantially burdened." The act provided that "government shall not burden a person's exercise of religion even if the burden results from a rule of general applicability [unless] it demonstrates that application of the burden . . . (1) furthers a compelling governmental interest, and (2) is the least restrictive means of furthering that compelling governmental interest."[24] President Clinton signed the act on November 16, 1993.

Four years later the Supreme Court, by a 6–3 vote, declared RFRA unconstitutional as applied to state and local governments in *City of Boerne v. Flores* (1997), on the ground that Congress had no authority to define the rights and privileges associated with the Fourteenth Amendment, since those interpretations were judicial functions rather than legislative prerogatives. Justice Kennedy explained that §5 gives Congress the power to enact laws "to enforce" the provisions of the Fourteenth Amendment, but that "Legislation which alters the meaning of the Free Exercise Clause cannot be said to be enforcing the Clause. Congress does not enforce a constitutional right by changing what the right is. It has been given the power 'to enforce,' not the power to determine what constitutes a constitutional violation. Were it not so, what Congress would be enforcing would no longer be, in any meaningful sense, the 'provisions of [the Fourteenth Amendment].' "[25]

Outraged by the Court's decision in *City of Boerne*, Congress enacted the Religious Land Use and Institutionalized Persons Act of 2000 (RLUIPA), which prohibits state and local government actions that impose a substantial burden on religious exercise in the treatment of institutionalized persons or in land use decisions, unless the government can prove these actions are the least restrictive means of furthering a compelling government interest.[26] Also, as of 2015, eighteen states passed their own Religious Freedom Restoration Acts, all of which require the state to meet strict scrutiny when substantially burdening religious freedom. Up until recently there has been very little litigation in these states, and most of the time religious plaintiffs have lost.[27]

The Supreme Court has assumed that RFRA can be applied to the actions of the federal government. For example, in 2006, in *Gonzales v. O Centro Espirita Beneficente Uniao do Vegetal*, the justices used strict scrutiny to protect a small religion that used a controlled substance in making a tea used in religious rituals, explaining that there was no compelling interest in preventing this small group from using the controlled substance in this way.[28] This was similar to the approach taken by the dissenters in *Smith*, who argued that the key question was not whether the government had a compelling interest in regulating controlled substances in general, but whether the application of those laws to these particular religious practitioners was supported by a compelling interest. In *Burwell v. Hobby Lobby* (2014), which we discuss in more detail later in this chapter, the Court held that it violates the Religious Freedom Restoration Act for the federal government to require that a closely held corporation provide insurance coverage for contraceptives that violates its owners' religious beliefs.[29]

The Theories Applied: Examples

In the realm of the Establishment Clause, the competing theories often lead to very different outcomes in individual cases, with the justices who embrace different theories often reaching very different results. The differences have been less stark in free exercise cases, especially given the historical record of the Court's use of strict scrutiny, which in practice resulted in very few protections for religious plaintiffs.[30]

Still, on their own terms, it is clear that the least protective approach would be one that assumed "belief but not conduct" is protected. More protective after that would be the *Smith* approach to protect belief and acts of worship against government action motivated by religious animus but would not protect religious observers who are incidentally (but perhaps seriously) burdened by neutral and general government policies. Most protective, at least in theory, would be the *Sherbert/Yoder* strict scrutiny approach that the Congress attempted to resurrect in RFRA, especially if it is used in a way that is more sensitive to religious claims and more demanding of compelling justifications from government, even when burdens on religion are indirect.

Still, this is not to say that the *Smith* approach would be incapable of offering meaningful protections for religious practitioners. Consider the case of *Church of the Lukumi Babalu Aye, Inc. v. City of Hialeah* (1993). The Santeria religion is a fusion of traditional African religious practices and Roman Catholicism. It originated in the 19th century when hundreds of thousands of members of the Yoruba people were brought as slaves from eastern Africa to Cuba. The Cuban Yoruba express their devotion to spirits, called *orishas*, through the iconography of Catholic saints. One of the principal forms of devotion is an animal sacrifice. Animals that are sacrificed include chickens, pigeons, doves, ducks, guinea pigs, goats, sheep, and turtles. The animals are killed by the cutting of the carotid arteries in the neck. Most of the time the sacrificed animals are then cooked and eaten.

After members of this church announced plans to open a church in the community of Hialeah, the city council held an emergency public session where it announced its "concern . . . that certain religions may propose to engage in practices which are inconsistent with public morals, peace or safety" and then approved a public ordinance that prohibited the unnecessary and cruel killing of animals. The council subsequently made it clear that religious sacrifice was cruel and unnecessary. The ordinances exempted slaughtering by licensed establishments.

If the Court adopted the "protect belief but not conduct" approach from *Reynolds* it would have been easy to uphold the government's actions. The Hialeah community was entitled to believe what it liked but had no right to engage in religious conduct that was inconsistent with the "social duties" imposed on everyone else in the community.

This case arose just a few years after *Smith* and a majority of the justices used the approach delineated in that case. Other justices believed that *Smith* was wrongly decided and that strict scrutiny was the more appropriate approach. How did these differences impact the justices' approach to the case?

Justice Kennedy wrote the opinion for the Court striking down the ordinances as unconstitutional. He considered it clear that "suppression of the central element of the Santeria worship was the object of the ordinances." Thus, the law was not a neutral attempt to promote a general secular purpose which just happened to impose an incidental burden on some religious practitioners. He made this point, not only with reference to the legislative history (including anti-sect statements at the council meetings), but also by pointing out that the ordinances created many exemptions for other types of animal killings—including exemptions for killing without the intent to use the animal for food, or killing with the intent to use the animal for food but without rituals, or ritualistic killing with the intent to use animals for food but using animals specifically raised for food purposes, which was designed to accommodate kosher butchering. These exemptions made it unlikely that the city was pursuing a neutral interest in the well-being of animals.

He added that "the legitimate governmental interests in protecting the public health and preventing cruelty to animals could be addressed by restrictions stopping far short of a flat prohibition of all Santeria sacrificial practice," for example, by focusing on adequate care of animals or proper disposal procedures.[31] In a passage that might be considered especially poignant in light of the Supreme Court's later decision to uphold President Donald Trump's so-called Muslim ban,[32] Kennedy summarized his view of the *Smith* approach this way:

> The Free Exercise Clause commits government itself to religious tolerance, and upon even slight suspicion that proposals for state intervention stem from animosity to religion or distrust of its practices, all officials must pause to remember their own high duty to the Constitution and to the rights it secures. Those in office must be resolute in resisting importunate demands and must ensure that the sole reasons for imposing the burdens of law and regulation are secular. Legislators may not

devise mechanisms, overt or disguised, designed to persecute or oppress a religion or its practices.

Under Kennedy's view of *Smith*, the Court must be on guard against government efforts to use the language of neutral and generalized laws as a pretext for religious animus—a kind of "strict scrutiny" of the foundational question of whether or not the law in question was in fact a neutral law of general applicability motivated by secular considerations.

Justices Scalia and Rehnquist agreed with the result, but disagreed with the reasons offered by Kennedy. In particular they wanted to emphasize that the key issue was that the law was not of general applicability and was thus not neutral. They wanted to distance themselves from the Court's review of the motives of the lawmakers, since they believe that "it is virtually impossible to determine the singular 'motive' of a collective legislative body," and thus the justices should focus exclusively on the language of the statute. Moreover, "The First Amendment does not refer to the purposes for which legislators enact laws, but to the effects of the laws enacted. . . . Had the Hialeah City Council set out resolutely to suppress the practices of Santeria, but ineptly adopted ordinances that failed to do so, I do not see how those laws could be said to 'prohibi[t] the free exercise' of religion. Nor, in my view, does it matter that a legislature consists entirely of the pure-hearted, if the law it enacts in fact singles out a religious practice for special burdens."

Justice Souter also wrote a separate opinion concurring in the outcome in order to indicate that he disagreed with the suggestion that the appropriate rule in this case was the one adopted in *Smith*. "The proposition for which the *Smith* rule stands . . . is that formal neutrality, along with general applicability, are sufficient conditions for constitutionality under the Free Exercise Clause. That proposition is not at issue in this case, however, for Hialeah's animal-sacrifice ordinances are not neutral under any definition, any more than they are generally applicable."

Souter then suggested that the Court should reexamine the *Smith* rule in the next case that would turn upon its application. He noted that *Smith* was inconsistent with the Court's settled commitment to using the compelling state interest test when examining laws that burdened religious practice. " 'Neutral, generally applicable' laws, drafted as they are from the perspective of the nonadherent, have the unavoidable potential of putting the believer to a choice between God and government. Our cases now present competing answers to the question when government, while pursuing secular ends, may compel disobedience to what one believes religion commands."

Blackmun and O'Connor also concurred separately "to empha-size that the First Amendment's protection of religion extends be-yond those rare occasions on which the government explicitly targets religion (or a particular religion) for disfavored treatment, as is done in this case. . . . I continue to believe that *Smith* was wrongly decided, because it ignored the value of religious freedom as an affirmative individual liberty and treated the Free Exercise Clause as no more than an antidiscrimination principle."[33]

In *Lukumi* there was little practical difference between applying strict scrutiny and the *Smith* standard, because both sides agreed that the township had explicitly targeted the practices of a disfavored re-ligion, while also going out of its way to accommodate other religious practices involving the killing of animals, such as kosher butchering. It raised the specter that a "more clever" city council might be able to draft oppressive laws that stayed within the boundaries estab-lished by *Smith*.

The differences in the approaches would have been more pro-nounced if we imagine a city with many citizens deeply concerned about the well-being of animals, which passes an ordinance banning the killing of animals except by licensed butchers or meat producers or by veterinarians performing medical euthanasia in a manner consistent with the ethics of their profession. Such a law might not be specifically targeted at religious practices, but it would impose a burden on members of the Santeria religion as well as some Muslim and Orthodox Jewish practices. If the justices who support *Smith* were convinced that such a law had a secular motivation and was not driven by religious animus, then it would be upheld despite its impact on certain religious practices. By contrast, as those justices who supported the *Sherbert/Yoder* approach signaled in their *Lukumi* dissents, they would likely have protected the Santeria practices even if the city council had not been specifically targeting the group, since "the First Amendment's protection of religion extends beyond those rare occasions on which the government explicitly targets religion" and because the Free Exercise Clause should be treated as something "more than an antidiscrimination principle."

To test the difference between *Smith* and *Sherbert/Yoder* we might also contemplate a general prohibition against the use of alcohol that did not provide accommodations for its sacramental uses. (During Prohibition the Congress did exempt the sacramental use of wine.) Under *Smith*, the only question would be whether the neutral law of general applicability was motivated by religious animus. If not, the law would be upheld as applied to religious practitioners, meaning that the government could penalize Catholics and Jews who use wine during services or religious observances at home, just as the *Smith* Court applied anti-drug laws against Native Americans who used peyote in religious settings. Under strict scrutiny, the key question would not be whether the government had an interest in prohibiting alcohol; it would be whether there was a separate compelling interest for enforcing that prohibition against those who use alcohol during worship or other religious observances.

To bring us back full circle, it is also helpful to consider the Court's first free exercise decision, *Reynolds v. United States*, in light of these more modern debates. Were federal laws criminalizing polygamy neutral laws of general application or were they motivated by religious animus? On the one hand, laws defining marriage as the union of one man and one woman were commonplace before the rise of Mormonism in the Anglo-American legal system. Then again, Congress's war on plural marriage in the territories began only after the settling of Mormons in the Utah territories, and by all accounts were drafted to specifically target the Utah Mormon Church, evincing a national intolerance toward Mormons and their practice of polygamy. A strict scrutiny analysis would need to be on guard against hidden religious animus and would need to assess whether there are compelling government interests independent of religious animus, such as concerns about protecting against sexual assault and incest and preventing fraud and failure to pay child support. One analyst concludes that (a) "If scrutinized under *Smith*, Utah's criminal bigamy statute would likely withstand constitutional scrutiny," (b) "No court has ever applied the *Lukumi* animus test to a statute simply because of historical context," but (c) "it is unlikely that a flat-out ban on polygamy would meet the 'least restrictive means' requirement of *Sherbert*."[34]

IN DEFENSE OF NO EXEMPTIONS FROM NEUTRAL LAWS OF GENERAL APPLICABILITY

We think that Justice Kennedy got it right in his *Lukumi* decision: Religious practitioners cannot claim exemptions from neutral laws of general applicability, but the Court should be on guard against efforts by government officials to offer secular justifications as pretexts for laws that are actually motivated by religious animus.

As with *Smith*, under this approach the Free Exercise Clause would prohibit efforts to punish or discriminate against people for their religious beliefs and would prohibit laws that target conduct associated with worship. By the same logic, this approach also recognizes what has been called the "Church Autonomy principle," which holds that "whenever the questions of discipline, or of faith, or ecclesiastical rule, custom or law have been decided by the highest of these church judicatories to which the matter has been carried, the legal tribunals must accept such decisions as final and binding on them, in their application of the case before them."[35] More generally this doctrine recognizes the right of religious institutions to select their clergy, control their doctrine, and determine how the organization is to be governed, without interference from the government.[36] There will always be controversies over how far the church autonomy principle should be extended—for example, if we allow religious institutions to discriminate on the basis of religion in hiring their clergy can they also discriminate when hiring religious school teachers or janitorial staff? But we believe the Free Exercise Clause should be interpreted to ensure that the internal operations of religious institutions with respect to doctrine, worship, and membership should be decided by religious practitioners and not by the government.

However, we agree with the *Smith* Court that neutral laws of general applicability may restrict matters of worship and even church autonomy. The right to build a church or school is subject to the ordinary laws that govern zoning and building. The right to conduct worship services is subject to general time, place, and manner restrictions governing all matters where groups organize themselves in public. Proselytizing is subjected to regular laws governing free speech, including, for example, laws that restrict all solicitations at a state fair to a fixed-booth location.[37] Relationships between clergy and laity are subject to the ordinary civil and criminal law, including laws protecting people from abuse or assault or requiring people to report crimes or refrain from participating in the cover-up of crimes.

As one scholar puts it, "Society is not duty bound by any constitutional right to let [religious entities] avoid duly enacted laws, especially where their actions can harm others. To say that religious liberty must encompass the right to harm others is to turn the First Amendment on its head."[38]

At the same time, *Lukumi* reveals that government officials hostile to religious practitioners rarely say explicitly that their regulations are motivated by religious animus. If religious practitioners should be required to acquiesce to neutral laws of general applicability, the Court should take care to ensure that the law is reasonably understood to arise from secular considerations of public policy.

There are five main reasons to prefer this approach to the *Sherbert/Yoder* strict scrutiny experiment.

First, if religious practitioners, but not others, may claim a right to be relieved of the ordinary social duties associated with a general law, then courts are immediately challenged with insoluble problems of distinguishing religious from non-religious objections. Formally organized religious institutions are easy enough to identify for purposes of prohibiting aid that would violate our understanding of the Establishment Clause—after all, those institutions are corporate entities with a designated tax status, have as their purpose the inculcation of religious values, and primarily employ and serve persons who share their religious tenets. But it is a different matter entirely to determine whether any individual's professed belief should qualify as distinctively religious and therefore deserving of special accommodation.[39]

Even at the birth of the nation, there was not total agreement on what religion meant. James Madison viewed religion as "the duty which we owe to our Creator and the Manner of discharging it," which is a view that excludes faiths that do not believe in a single creator, or a creator at all. Thomas Jefferson apparently envisioned religious liberty for various faiths. Jefferson stated that his Virginia

Act for Establishing Religious Freedom "was meant to be universal . . . to comprehend within the mantle of its protection the Jew and the Gentile, the Christian and Mohometan, the Hindu, and infidel of every denomination."[40] This would be a broader approach than Madison's and would allow religion to mean many things and apply to almost everyone. But such an approach would not be helpful to those who argue that religious people, but not others, should be granted special accommodations to general laws that incidentally burden their beliefs. Moreover, a broad definition of religion—for example, one that would treat a commitment to science as a kind of religion—would make Establishment Clause decision making impossible, since almost anything government did (e.g., teach science in schools) would have to be considered an establishment of religion.

No Supreme Court decision has attempted to define the meaning of "religion" in the First Amendment but has addressed the question when interpreting the scope of a religious exemption to the Selective Service Act, which authorized the military draft. In *United States v. Seeger* (1965), the Court construed a provision of the Universal Military Training and Selective Service Act that exempted for combat training and service in the armed forces those individuals "who by reason of their religious training and belief are conscientiously opposed to participation in war in any form." The law defined "religious training and belief" as "an individual's belief in relation to a Supreme Being involving duties superior to those arising from any human relation, but [not including] essentially political, sociological, or philosophical views or a merely personal moral code." *Seeger* involved an individual who sought a religious exemption from the draft, but denied any belief in a Supreme Being.

The Court broadly defined religion to include such nontheistic views. The Court said: "We believe that . . . the test of belief 'in a relation to a Supreme Being' is whether a given belief that is sincere and meaningful occupies a place in the life of its possessor parallel to that filled by the orthodox belief in God of one who clearly qualifies for the exemption."[41] The Court, however, offered no criteria for assessing whether a particular view is religious under this definition. Nor did the Court do so in the subsequent case of *Welsh v. United States* (1970). Again, the Court said that the crucial inquiry "in determining whether the registrant's beliefs are religious is whether these beliefs play the role of a religion and function as a religion in the registrant's life."[42] Yet this does not seem a useful approach. How is a court to decide whether a view occupies the place in a person's life that religion does for a religious person?

It is impossible to formulate a definition of religion that encompasses the vast array of spiritual beliefs and practices that are present in the United States.[43] As one commentator noted, "There is no single characteristic or set of characteristics that all religions have in common that makes them religions."[44] Moreover, any attempt to define religion raises concerns that choosing a single definition is itself an establishment of religion. We agree that many constitutional concepts are difficult to define—the meanings of "search and seizure," "equal protection," and "cruel and unusual" have been debated from the beginning. But to adopt an approach to free exercise that requires the government to make an official decision about whether an individual person's belief deserves the label "religious" raises insoluble Establishment Clause challenges and inevitably requires the government to elevate some spiritual communities over others. The approach we advocate creates far fewer situations where courts become entangled in such issues.

Second, even when courts might be confident that they are dealing with religious claims, the strict scrutiny approach would obligate them to determine the importance or centrality of the religious claim. Are the claimed burdens sincerely expressed? Are the burdens serious or trivial? Elements of burden, sincerity, and religiosity are central to the strict scrutiny formula and inevitably entangle government officials in basic matters of religious faith and practice. If the members of a Native American family report that they have recently reached the conclusion that the very idea of social security numbers are inconsistent with tenets of their religion, should such claims always be taken at face value? If a defendant in a prostitution prosecution claims she is a leader of the Church of the Most High Goddess, and it is church doctrine that people earn "absolution" through sex and "sacrifice" through a payment of money, should that be taken at face value?[45] As one scholar put it, "Behind every free exercise claim is a spectral march; grant this one, a voice whispers to each judge, and you will be confronted with an endless chain of exemption demands from religious deviants of every stripe."[46]

When Christian parents complained that the public school reading curriculum impermissibly burdened their religious beliefs, which compelled them to refrain from exposure to non-Christian ideas, the strict scrutiny approach required the Court of Appeals to reach a conclusion whether or not such exposure actually imposed a burden on their religion. Chief Judge Lively concluded that the reading requirements did not amount to a significant enough burden, since the children were obliged only to read the challenged material, not to affirm the truth of what they read. When an imprisoned Wiccan claimed under RLUIPA that his religious exercise was burdened by the state's restriction on his practice of faith outdoors, using a variety of artifacts, the court refused to offer an accommodation in part because prison officials consulted with their own expert on Wiccan practice, who opined that the faith did not require what the prisoner wanted.[47] It is deeply disturbing to have a government official tell religious practitioners what their faith requires, yet such a conclusion is inherent in the enterprise of strict scrutiny. This approach is therefore also in tension with one of the most important statements of constitutional principle in the Supreme Court's case law, namely, that "if there is a fixed star in our constitutional constellation, it is that no official, high or petty, can prescribe what shall be orthodox in politics, nationalism, religion, or other matters of opinion."[48] Abandoning the need to provide accommodations obviates the need to define religion or assess the weightiness of religious claims, and avoiding such judgments by government officials is a vital component of the protection of religious freedom. This alone is reason enough to abandon the strict scrutiny approach.[49]

Third, a constitutional obligation to grant special exemptions gives undue favoritism to people with religious convictions over people with similarly strong secular convictions, in contravention of the fundamental commitment to ensure a secular American government. It is not only Native Americans who may be deeply concerned that it is dehumanizing to reduce a person to a social security number. Not only the Amish object to mandatory education laws. People other than conservative Christians may believe that public schools are teaching material that is inconsistent with their strongly held beliefs. In *Thomas v. Review Board* (1981) the Court allowed for unemployment benefits for a Jehovah's Witness who quit his job at Blaw-Knox Foundry & Machinery Company after it transferred all of its operations to weapons manufacturing.[50] The Court was clear that Eddie C. Thomas should get unemployment benefits because of his religious beliefs; the justices were also clear that a person who quit based on non-religious moral grounds would not be entitled to those benefits. But on what grounds should Eddie Thomas's conscience be given superior consideration to the conscience of a pacifist atheist?

Some believe that the Constitution itself insists on this preference by extending special protections to the free exercise of religion. But as we have discussed in Chapter 2, there is nothing in the language or tradition of the Free Exercise Clause that should lead the government to prefer religious belief over non-religious belief when it comes to the question of which individuals are bound by the ordinary social duties imposed on everyone.[51] The founders wanted people to be free to organize themselves into religious communities, but they did not assume that religious people did not have to obey laws that others had to obey. The framers wanted to avoid the political turmoil and violence associated with governments that were closely aligned with particular religions, and to guard against religious oppression. There is no evidence that, in the drafting of the Constitution or Bill of Rights, they were intending to ensure the primacy of religious beliefs and activities over other beliefs and activities. The decision to prohibit religious tests for office, for example, was designed to ensure that there would be no religious favoritism in one's ability to represent the people. Rather than favor religion over non-religion, the Constitution embodies a vision of a secular government that is neutral with respect to religion. This is why "various justices have taken the view that free exercise exemptions are establishment clause violations, because the exempting government agent creates a preference for religious over comparable nonreligious experience."[52]

To give religious belief and conduct a special place, one would need to establish that religion is "unique form of public and social identity, involving a vast plurality of sanctuaries, schools, charities, missions, and other forms and forums of faith."[53] There was undoubtedly a time when many people believed this was so, but the claim cannot be maintained within our more religiously diverse and secular society. The "hundreds of millions of people who have no religious beliefs presumably still have individual and personal identities, defined by sundry other systems of belief," and for many people "politics, class, ethnicity, cultural traditions, and so on" are experienced as much more central to public and social identity than religious affiliation.[54] It may be true that some laws put religious adherents in the unwelcome position of being subjected to conflicting duties. But this is also true of non-religious people, who also feel compelled by moral or political duties. And there is no reason to believe that there is a special suffering associated with the violation of a religious tenet, especially since not all religious tenets are held with equal fervor and not all religious beliefs are necessarily more deeply felt that secular beliefs.

Fourth, a commitment to accommodate the beliefs and conduct of religious practitioners whenever there is no "compelling state interest" creates impossible expectations, especially in light of the tremendous diversity of religious faith and practice in modern America, with the most likely result being a pattern of decisions that are arbitrary, ill-informed, ad hoc, or politically charged.[55] At a time when the population was associated with a relatively small number of familiar faith traditions, and the government was less involved in legislation and regulation, it might be imaginable to treat religious accommodation as a manageable aspiration. But we now live in a time of extraordinary religious diversity, of both theistic and nontheistic faith traditions, with some strongly associated with temples, churches, or sanctuaries and others associated with relationships to nature and other humans. All of this adds up to an uncountable number of practices considered religious duties, including refusals to obtain social security numbers and bringing a *kirpan* (daggar or sword) to school when a Sikh male turns fourteen.[56] Moreover, the modern American state touches every aspect of our lives and imposes a wide range of social duties relating to taxes, military service, medical care, insurance coverage, workplace health and safety, child welfare, vaccinations, controlled substances, wages, animal cruelty, environmental protection, anti-discrimination, zoning—the list is endless. In other words, there is an "enormous range of legal norms that may fall prey to religious exemption claims" since they implicate "a range of religious beliefs and practices as wide and deep as the human condition itself, and a correspondingly broad range of government interests."[57]

The idea that, in this environment, no religious person should be at all disadvantaged or burdened with respect to that person's spiritual beliefs and practices is an impossible aspiration, with the likely outcome being either that no accommodations can be made for fear of an unmanageable slippery slope or that only mainstream, familiar, or otherwise favored practitioners will be taken seriously (just consider the outcomes in *Reynolds*, *Yoder*, and *Lyng*). We acknowledge that some religious practitioners are less likely to feel the incidental burden of government action because their more mainstream position ensures more sensitivity among legislators. But there is no way to equalize the playing field so that all religious practitioners experience the same distribution of burdens and benefits, and the downsides of judicial efforts to ensure such equality outweigh the theoretical benefits from such an attempt. The only way that people of strong religious faith and fealty will not feel burdened or frustrated at the larger political culture is to live in a theocracy of their choosing, and even then there are sure to be frustrations. The feeling that one's strongly held views or preferred conduct is not adequately respected in law is commonplace and inevitable among people who live in diverse, representative polities. The refusal to take extraordinary steps to mitigate every possible burden is no sign of disrespect for the religious; it simply places the religious on the same footing as everyone else.

Fifth, the strict scrutiny approach, when tried, did not turn out well. As discussed earlier, during the 27-year experiment between *Sherbert* and *Smith*, there were only two narrow areas where any special exemptions or accommodations were considered justified. After *Smith*, Congress attempted to reinstate the presumptively more protective *Sherbert/Yoder* standard, but up until recently even that has not proved impactful. In fact, the federal RFRA has frequently been criticized as ineffective.[58] State RFRAs were also passed in the wake of *Smith* but most have been narrowly construed and there has been little of interest in the resulting judicial decision making.[59] We cannot say with confidence why decades of experience with formal constitutional tests that demanded more serious protections have proved relatively ineffectual. We suspect that there are inherent problems with religious entanglement and slippery slope arguments that make judges cautious. The point, though, is that there is good reason to think that the benefits of a serious strict scrutiny approach may be less impactful than one might assume when it comes to more robust protection for a wide array for religious minorities. The more likely outcome of such an approach would be more robust protections for politically powerful or mainstream religions rather than a more equal playing field for all religious practitioners. This, combined with the serious concerns and complications previously mentioned, should lead us to be deeply suspicious about whether such an approach can accomplish what its advocates imagine. In other words, the benefits of a *Sherbert/Yoder* approach may be less obvious than one would assume, even while the costs or complications are clearly more serious than what we see with a *Smith*-like approach.

Our approach fully protects "the rights of the people to maintain their own choices of religious experience," limited only "by restraints that flow from the government's secular character and the disabilities that flow from that character."[60] There are some who suggest that a more appropriate approach would be to offer exemptions to religious practitioners when accommodations have costs that are "minimal and widely shared"[61] or when the burdens on third parties are trivial.[62] This is attractive if we are especially bothered by circumstances where accommodations appear to us to be harmless yet meaningful to the faithful, as with the hypothetical case of a prohibition law that does not contemplate exceptions for the religious use of wine as a sacrament during worship services, or a military psychologist wearing a yarmulke while on duty at a military hospital, or a Muslim prisoner requesting an exemption from his prison's no-beards policy for a one-half inch beard.[63]

We acknowledge that our approach will result in some religious practitioners being burdened by neutral laws of general applicability. However, this will be true under any approach as evidenced by the many cases that rejected free exercise claims even when the Court was ostensibly following *Sherbert v. Verner.* Moreover, we believe that our approach ensures greater religious liberty overall, risks fewer ad hoc and discriminatory judgments by courts, avoids government entanglement with basic questions of religious doctrine and practice, and prevents real harms and burdens that would be caused if religious practitioners were exempt from laws that promote public health, safety, and morality. Among other things, what some people view as "minimal" or "trivial" harms or burdens on third parties is viewed by others very differently. It is not clear whether the *Yoder* Court properly assessed the harm to Amish children, or whether instead the Court had political or ideological reasons for accommodating the Amish in a way they would not accommodate other religious practitioners. Scholars are also increasingly viewing relevant third-party harms very broadly, to encompass not only concrete physical harms, of the sort we might associate with the denial of medical treatment, but also dignity harms, such as those suffered by historically disadvantaged groups who find themselves targeted by religious practitioners seeking exceptions from general anti-discrimination laws. There is no reason to think that judges are uniquely well qualified to decide whether it is better to honor the interests of religious business people who do not want to sell to gay or lesbian customers or honor the rights of the LGBTQ community not to be discriminated against by people engaged in commerce.

Finally, under our approach, courts would be on guard against facial claims of neutral government interests that are masking religious animus. After all, what precisely is the neutral government interest in not allowing Muslim prisoners to have half-inch beards when the prison allows quarter-inch beards and allows prisoners to shave mustaches and head hair?[64]

What would it mean for the Court to focus free exercise claims on prohibitions against targeted animus but not provide exemptions to neutral laws of general applicability? Consider two examples that capture much of the recent debate over religious liberty: the duty of religious employers or providers to follow general laws regarding access to adequate health insurance or health services, and the question of whether a business owner, based on her or his religious beliefs, may refuse to serve clients because of their religious objection to same-sex practices.

Religious Employers and Laws Governing Employee Benefits

We believe that religious practitioners outside of church settings should not be able to use free exercise claims as a basis for denying medical care or insurance coverage to others. But advocates for religious freedom have been fighting for the recognition of such a right for years now.

When the Patient Protection and Affordable Care Act (ACA) was passed in March 2010 it mandated that group health plans, including self-insured plans (in which an employer is the insurer), cover the cost of preventive care for women, including coverage for contraceptives. In the wake of objections that covering contraception would violate some employers' religious freedoms, interim rules were published in 2011 announcing that churches, but not religiously affiliated groups such as religious schools or hospitals, would be exempt from the mandate. To qualify the church would have to be a nonprofit recognized under the Internal Revenue Code, have as its purpose the inculcation of religious values, and primarily employ and serve persons who share its religious tenets. This accommodation of churches was not considered sufficient by religious objectors to the ACA. So in 2012 the Obama Administration indicated that religious not-for-profit employers such as hospitals, universities, and charities would not have to pay for contraceptives themselves, but instead would have their insurance providers pay for the services.[65] Many religious organizations again complained that this was not a sufficient accommodation, because it required religious employers to be complicit in behavior that they believed to be morally wrong.[66]

These objections eventually arrived on the doorstep of the Supreme Court in the case *Burwell v. Hobby Lobby Stores, Inc.* (2014). David Green, Barbara Green, and their three children owned Hobby Lobby, a chain of 500 stores with 13,000 employees, as a "closely held for-profit" corporation (similar to several million other corporations). They claimed that the Free Exercise Clause and the Religious Freedom Restoration Act required the federal government to exempt them from the duty to provide preventive health care for women, including contraceptives. Of course, no one was claiming that they were being forced to use contraceptives against their will, or that they were denied the right to pray about the evils of contraceptives, or that they were being stopped from speaking out against contraception or abortion. They were merely objecting to being required to take an action as an employer of a diverse range of people that might enable their workers to do things that are at odds with the owners' religious beliefs.

For the first time in American history, the Supreme Court, using the strict scrutiny standard required under RFRA, held that religious freedom included a right to deny other people benefits to which they would otherwise be entitled to if they did not have a religious employer. Writing for a 5-4 majority Justice Alito first ruled that corporations should be considered "persons" who are entitled to assert rights of religious liberty—a deeply problematic understanding of the "rights" of a fictional entity that (needless to say) is not capable of having a religion or engaging in religious practice. By allowing the owners to attribute their beliefs to this separate entity the Court also held that employers who were engaged in ordinary nonreligious commercial activities could be exempted from the same rules that applied to everyone else engaged in commerce if they had religious objections to how their non-religious employees might use their health benefits.

Justice Alito assumed for the sake of argument that the ACA requirements were "compelling" and then turned to the question of whether the mandate is "the least restrictive means of furthering that compelling government interest." He declared that this "exceptionally demanding" standard "is not satisfied here" because the government "has not shown that it lacks other means of achieving its desired goal without imposing a substantial burden on the exercise of religion by the objecting parties . . . " Alito noted that the government had already established accommodations for religious not-for-profit organizations, whereby the organization "can self-certify that it opposes providing coverage" for these services, leading to a scheme whereby the government can assume the costs. "We do not decide today whether an approach of this type complies with RFRA for purposes of all religious claims," but at a minimum "it does not impinge on the plaintiff's religious belief that providing insurance coverage for the contraceptives at issue here violates their religion. . . ." Note that the Court accepted at face value the plaintiff's claims that the requirement impinges on their beliefs, and then transforms that religious belief objection into a "substantial burden on the exercise of religion" of the offended believers— meaning that a religious disagreement with a government policy, even in a commercial setting implicating nothing about matters of worship, prayer, and the like, is treated as "impinging" on the free exercise of religion.

In her dissent, Justice Ginsburg disagreed that this case involves a substantial burdening of religious belief or conduct. She noted that the law "carries no command" that religious employers "purchase or provide the contraceptives they find objectionable." As with all employer-based health insurance, the companies "direct money into undifferentiated funds that finance a wide variety of benefits under comprehensive health plans," and "any decision to use contraceptives made by a woman covered under Hobby Lobby's . . . plan will not be propelled by the Government, it will be the woman's autonomous choice, informed by the physician she consults." The employer is no more involved in the decision to use contraceptives than they would be involved in an employee's decision to use his salary to purchase liquor, gamble, or engage in other behaviors that the owners might consider sinful.

The dissent also noted the "startling breadth" of a ruling that so blatantly disregarded the "disadvantages that religion-based opt-outs impose on others" and that so casually held that the "least restrictive alternative" requirement might be triggered if one could imagine an entirely different regulatory scheme that solved the problem by having "the general public . . . pick up the tab." She noted that "religious organizations exist to foster the interests of persons subscribing to the same religious faith," but this is not the case with "for-profit corporations," that have workers who "are not drawn from one religious community. . . . The distinction between a community made up of believers in the same religion and one embracing persons of diverse beliefs, clear as it is, constantly escapes the Court's attention."

She then asked, "where is the stopping point to the 'let the government pay' alternative?"

Suppose an employer's sincerely held religious belief is offended by health coverage of vaccines, or paying the minimum wage, or according women equal pay for substantially similar work? Does it rank as a less restrictive alternative to require the government to provide the money or benefit to which the employer has a religion-based objection? . . . [What of] employers with religiously grounded objections to blood transfusions (Jehovah's Witnesses); antidepressants (Scientologists); medications derived from pigs, including anesthesia, intravenous fluids, and pills coated with gelatin (certain Muslims, Jews, and Hindus); and vaccinations (Christian Scientists, among others)?

Justice Ginsburg argued that "There is an overriding interest . . . in keeping the courts 'out of the business of evaluating the relative merits of differing religious claims,' or the sincerity with which an asserted religious belief is held. Indeed, approving some religious claims while deeming others unworthy of accommodation could be 'perceived as favoring one religion over another,' the very 'risk the Establishment Clause was designed to preclude.' The Court, I fear, has ventured into a minefield." Consequently, she concluded that it would be more appropriate for the Court to "confine religious exemptions [under RFRA] to organizations formed 'for a religious purpose,' 'engage[d] primarily in carrying out that religious purpose,' and not 'engaged . . . substantially in the exchange of goods or services for money beyond nominal amounts.'"[67]

Our view is entirely consistent with Justice Ginsburg's approach. We believe it is appropriate to give formally recognized religious institutions latitude to determine the internal workings of their organizational structure, especially as they relate to the employment of people directly engaged in matters of religious faith, instruction, and worship. The federal government should not be telling churches, mosques, and synagogues who can be priests, imams, and rabbis. The demands on their private behavior are also matters of religious doctrine and practice. But outside this sphere, people who happen to be religious who are otherwise active in not-for-profit or for-profit non-religious–focused activity—including medical care or general commercial enterprises—have no religious freedom rights to assert against the general regulatory structures that govern (for example) hospital care or employee relations. The logic of the majority opinion would seem to allow Christian Science employers to refuse to provide any health insurance to employees, or allow any religious employer who opposes contraceptives to require as a condition of employment that their employees will not use their salary to purchase contraceptives or access abortions.[68] It is impossible, given the majority's reasoning, to explain why an Orthodox Jewish or observant Muslim employer could not insist that none of the salary paid could be used to buy pork products.

A better approach to these issues was taken by the Ninth Circuit in assessing whether religious pharmacy owners and pharmacists were entitled under the Free Exercise Clause to refuse to fill prescriptions of medications when their religious beliefs opposed the use of the medications—in this case, emergency contraceptives such as Plan B. Because the policies at issue involved the state of Washington and not the federal government the judges used the *Smith* standard to assess the competing claims, and denied the arguments of the religious pharmacists on the grounds that the law was neutral and of general applicability. The pharmacists' religious objections did not matter in the face of state regulations designed to ensure that patients have safe and timely access to their lawfully prescribed medications.[69] Even though the Congress that enacted RFRA rejected the *Smith* standard, we believe this approach is the more appropriate even in the federal setting.

This is the same logic that does, and should, require parents to provide necessary medical care to their children even if their religious beliefs obligate them to instead rely on the power of prayer. The logic supports the obligation of doctors to meet the standard of care even in cases where they have religious objections to how same-sex couples might use assisted reproductive technologies; and it supports mandatory vaccination laws even over religious objections, both because of their impact on the well-being of a child but also because of the larger public health interest in a high percentage of vaccinated people.[70] Simply put, free exercise of religion does not mean that people, in following their religious beliefs, can violate general laws and inflict injuries on others.

This is why it was appropriate for a federal district court judge in the Fall of 2019 to void the Trump administration's "conscience rule," which would have made it easier for health care workers to avoid assisting with abortion or other medical procedures on religious grounds–with hospitals, insurance companies, or local governments facing a loss of federal funds if they were deemed in violation of their employees' rights under the rule. The case was brought by 19 states, three cities, a county, and two reproductive health providers who expressed concern that the rule would prevent vulnerable patients from obtaining needed care. During the oral argument, Judge Paul A. Engelmayer asked a Justice Department lawyer whether an ambulance driver with objections to abortion could choose to not transport a pregnant woman to a hospital if he discovered that she was headed there to terminate an ectopic pregnancy. The government's lawyer responded that the conscience rule would give the ambulance driver such a right. That cannot be the best way to think about the proper scope of religious liberty.[71]

In the spring of 2020, the issue of the exception to the contraceptive mandate was again before the Supreme Court in *Little Sisters of the Poor Saint Peters and Paul Home v. Pennsylvania*[72] and *Trump v. Pennsylvania*.[73] The Patient Protection and Affordable Care Act requires that employers provide health insurance that includes contraceptive coverage for their female employees. Under federal regulations, religious institutions were exempted from having to do this. Not-for-profit institutions affiliated with religions could opt out and insurance carriers then would provide coverage. But other employers had to provide this coverage. As described above, in *Hobby Lobby v. Burwell*, the Court held that it violated the Religious Freedom Restoration Act to require that a close corporation provide contraceptive coverage if it violates its owners religious beliefs.

In 2016, the Court heard oral arguments as to whether the opt-out for not-for-profit affiliates with religious institutions violated RFRA by making them complicit in the provision of contraceptives that violated their religious beliefs. The Court did not decide the issue, likely because it was split 4-4 after Justice Scalia's death. Instead the Court sent the cases back to the lower courts with instructions for the federal government and the challengers to try to work out a solution that would allow female employees to receive full contraceptive coverage while still respecting the employers' religious beliefs.

In 2017, the Trump administration issued new rules that expanded the exemption from the contraceptive mandate and permitted private employers with religious or moral objections to the mandate to opt out of providing contraceptive coverage for their women employees. New Jersey and Pennsylvania sued and contended that this violated the Affordable Care Act and was done in a manner inconsistent with the Administrative Procedures Act because there was no opportunity for notice and comment rulemaking. The district court ruled in favor in favor of the states and the United States Court of Appeals for the Third Circuit affirmed.

The precise questions before the Court are not about religious freedom; they concern interpreting the Affordable Care Act and administrative law. But the underlying issue is the question of whether the government can force employers to provide contraceptive coverage that violates the employers' beliefs. As we argue above, laws requiring this of all employers should be upheld and there should not be exemptions for religious or religiously affiliated institutions.

Religious Business Owners and Anti-Discrimination Laws

The ACA triggered conservative religious freedom activism with respect to the rights of religious employers and related issues involving access to medical care. Similarly, the rapid transformation of American law extending rights to the LGBTQ (lesbian, gay, bisexual, transgender, and queer or questioning) community, including the right to same-sex marriage, triggered a backlash by religious conservatives who did not want to support a practice that they object to on religious grounds.[74] "Examples include innkeepers and restaurant owners who do not want to host same-sex weddings, bakers and florists who do not want to provide their services for such weddings, employers who do not want to extend family health benefits to married same-sex couples, and landlords and hotel owners who do not want to rent apartments or rooms to such couples."[75]

Under our approach, clergy who have religious objections to same-sex marriage are not required to perform such ceremonies, because that strikes at the core of the exercise of their religion. Churches, synagogues, and mosques are not required to make their facilities available for same-sex weddings if such weddings violate the religious doctrines and practices of particular sects and denominations. However, when religious people are engaged in ordinary callings and participate in commerce, they are obligated to follow the same rules that apply to everyone else who is similarly situated, including fidelity to anti-discrimination laws. As one scholar put it in discussing whether religious objections to interracial marriage or civil rights would allow religious persons to be exempt from civil rights legislation, the "internal affairs of churches are an enclave where the free exercise clause must control," but "outside such enclaves, the policy against racial discrimination controls." For example,

> A religiously motivated citizen who is conscientiously opposed to racial equality encounters legally required nondiscrimination almost everywhere he goes. . . . If he owns a business, he must hire and service all races on an equal basis. If he buys or sells property, he must deal with blacks and whites on equal terms. His objection to racial equality does not entitle him to be excused from these obligations; when he participates in government or the secular economy, he must obey the secular rules that apply to all.[76]

These views were expressed in 1982. More recently, this same scholar, Douglas Laycock, argued in favor of a stronger strict scrutiny approach when the religious objection was to same-sex marriage: "The scope of any right to refuse service to same-sex couples must depend on comparing the harm to the couple of being refused service and the harm to the merchant or service provider of being coerced to provide service. . . . In my view, the right to one's own moral integrity should generally trump the inconvenience of having to get the same service from another provider nearby."[77]

We believe the approach that Laycock articulated 1982 is also appropriate for current debates about how religious arguments cannot be allowed to justify discrimination against same-sex couples. In the secular world, people encounter disagreements of conscience all the time, but they are not granted exemptions to neutral laws of general applicability. The sort of balancing associated with "comparing the harm[s]" has already been undertaken in the legislation, and it is not possible for courts to resolve these issues in any way other than by choosing favored religions and disregarding the public interests associated with legislation protecting against discrimination.[78] It is a chilling reminder of the similarities between civil rights for same-sex couples and civil rights for African Americans when we see a modern city council member defend a decision to discriminate against a black job applicant by explaining, "I'm a Christian and my Christian beliefs are you don't do interracial marriage. . . . [W]hen you see blacks and whites together, it makes my blood boil because that's just not the way a Christian is supposed to live."[79] How, exactly, would those who advocate exceptions for religious practitioners assess this claim? By denying it is a religiously sincere belief? By concluding it is not really a central belief of this person's faith? By concluding that eradicating discrimination against same-sex couples is less important than eradicating discrimination against African Americans?

Most of the arguments for accommodating religious objectors who are operating in civil society emphasize that the same "dignity loss" felt by same-sex couples who are refused otherwise available services are also felt by religious people "who are told that their beliefs are not to be tolerated, at least not in the public sphere."[80] But this is an overheated use of the word "tolerated." The government is not seeking to take any action against individuals merely because they hold particular beliefs; holding such beliefs is tolerated. The religious objectors are free to advocate different policies, and there is no shortage of religious advocacy against same-sex marriage or other actions that violate their understanding of moral behavior.[81] These efforts are tolerated. Objectors are free to worship and pray in a manner that reflects their views of who should be considered a sinner. What is not "tolerated" is simply the idea that they are entitled to have their religious views always be reflected in civil law or that they are entitled to be exempted from civic duties that conflict with their views. But no one is so entitled.

Another version of the argument in favor of granting exemptions is that the religious objectors do not want to be "complicit" in assertedly sinful conduct of others.[82] Just as religious employers believe that the requirement to provide contraceptive services in health plans directly involves them in the use of contraceptives, religious wedding photographers, wedding cake makers, and flower suppliers have argued that the requirement that they provide services as part of a same-sex wedding ceremony makes them directly involved in an activity they consider sinful, and it is this complicity that raises fundamental religious liberty claims.[83] But this is an overheated use of the concept "complicit." Choosing to obey a legally required social duty does not morally implicate a person in all behaviors linked to that social duty. Paying taxes does not make pacifists complicit in military adventurism or libertarians complicit in expanded government regulation. Paying an employee a salary does not make the employer complicit in all the ways in which a person spends the money.

In addition, it is hard to see the limiting principle if one claimed a constitutional right to do nothing that would facilitate the existence of same-sex marriages. If increasing numbers of states extended civil rights and public accommodations protections to people on the basis of gender identity and sexual orientation, religious people could, in principle, refuse to sell houses or rent apartments to same-sex married couples, or refuse to sell groceries to them, or employ them, or provide them any goods or services.

We believe that the Supreme Court of New Mexico got it right when it decided in *Elane Photography, LLC v. Willock* that a wedding photography business violated the state's human rights act when it refused to photograph a same-sex commitment ceremony. The act prohibited businesses that sell services to the general public from discriminating against people based on their sexual orientation. In assessing the free exercise claims, the Court noted that the state's human rights act was "a neutral law of general applicability" because, even though it has some exceptions (for example, for individuals who live in small dwellings and rent out rooms in their units), those exceptions "apply equally to religious and secular conduct" and there is no indication of "any animus toward religion by the Legislature." The statute also allowed "religious organizations" to serve only or primarily people of their own faith, but those restrictions do not apply when religious organizations sell goods or services to the general public. These exemptions for religious organizations "are common in a wide variety of laws, and they reflect the attempt of the Legislature to respect free exercise rights by reducing burdens on religion," but they "do not prefer secular conduct over religious conduct or evince any hostility toward religion."[84]

We also agree with the approach adopted by the Supreme Court of Washington when it reached a similar decision in a case involving a flower shop owner. The court noted that the state's anti-discrimination laws contained express exemptions for religious organizations—with the law stating that "no religious organization is required to provide accommodations, facilities, advantages, privileges, services, or goods related to the solemnization or celebration of marriage"—but this was a limited recognition of the core free exercise rights of religious organizations, not the rights of entities that serve the public more generally in public commercial settings. The court noted that there is no indication that the legislature "intended to import a fact-specific, case-by-case, constitutional balancing test" in assessing the interests of religious business owners and customers; moreover, in many other contexts "this court and the United States Supreme Court have held that individuals who engage in commerce necessarily accept some limitations on their conduct as a result."[85]

The only opportunity that the Supreme Court has had to weigh in on this particular issue was in *Masterpiece Cakeshop, Ltd. v. Colorado Civil Rights Commission* (2018),[86] and the results were inconclusive.

Charlie Craig and David Mullins got married in Massachusetts and wanted to celebrate their wedding where they lived in Colorado. They went to a local bakery, Masterpiece Cakeshop, a limited liability company in Colorado, and sought to purchase a wedding cake. Jack Phillips, the owner of Denver's Masterpiece Cakes, refused to bake wedding cakes for same-sex couples because he "believes that the Bible commands him . . . not to encourage sin in any way" and that the baking of the cake would force him to "participate" in the sinful ceremony.[87] He was willing for his bakery to sell an already prepared cake for the couple, but not to make one for them. The Colorado Civil Rights Commission found that Phillips violated Colorado's public accommodations law that prohibits business establishments from discriminating, including on the basis of sexual orientation. Phillips would design and bake a cake for opposite-sex couples, but not for same-sex couples, a form of discrimination that violated state law.

The Supreme Court reversed in a 7–2 decision. Justice Kennedy wrote for the Court; only Justices Ginsburg and Sotomayor dissented. Justice Kennedy framed the case as presenting "difficult questions as to the proper reconciliation of at least two principles": the authority of the state to protect the rights and dignity of gay persons who wish to be married but face discrimination when they seek goods and services, and the right of religious persons to exercise their fundamental freedoms under the First Amendment. He noted that details matter; for example, it might be different if a cakeshop owner refused to create a specialized cake where he was asked to write a particular message on a cake versus whether he refused to sell an off-the-shelf cake to people because of the nature of their celebration. Kennedy also noted that "the baker, in his capacity as the owner of a business serving the public, might have his right to the free exercise of religion limited by generally applicable laws." But he was particularly concerned that, in this case, the "question of when the free exercise of his religion must yield to an otherwise valid exercise of state power needed to be determined in an adjudication in which religious hostility on the part of the State itself would not be a factor in the balance the State sought to reach."

In other words, while bakers have to follow neutral laws of general applicability, the Court concluded that there was evidence of religious animus in the way the state assessed the baker's claim. Justice Kennedy wrote: "The Civil Rights Commission's treatment of his case has some elements of a clear and impermissible hostility toward the sincere religious beliefs that motivated his objection." The Court especially focused on a statement made by a commissioner at a subsequent meeting: "Freedom of religion and religion has been used to justify all kinds of discrimination throughout history, whether it be slavery, whether it be the holocaust, whether it be—I mean, we—we can list hundreds of situations where freedom of religion has been used to justify discrimination. And to me it is one of the most despicable pieces of rhetoric that people can use to—to use their religion to hurt others."

Justice Kennedy said that this was "disparaging" to religion and thus showed hostility. He wrote:

> To describe a man's faith as 'one of the most despicable pieces of rhetoric that people can use' is to disparage his religion in at least two distinct ways: by describing it as despicable, and also by characterizing it as merely rhetorical—something insubstantial and even insincere. The commissioner even went so far as to compare Phillips' invocation of his sincerely held religious beliefs to defenses of slavery and the Holocaust. This sentiment is inappropriate for a Commission charged with the solemn responsibility of fair and neutral enforcement of Colorado's antidiscrimination law—a law that protects against discrimination on the basis of religion as well as sexual orientation.

The Court did not speculate what the outcome might be if there was no evidence of religious animus, but in the face of such evidence a majority decided that the state's actions violated the Free Exercise Clause.

While we agree that the Court should guard against state action that is based on animus toward religion, we disagree that these statements reflect a kind of animus that violates the Constitution. The phrase that was most concerning to the Court expressed the opinion that it is wrong to use religion as a basis for hurting others and especially to justify discrimination. That observation in and of itself does not reflect animus against religion; it explains why the invocation of religion is not a reason to allow individuals to disregard laws that are designed to extend civil rights protections to historically disadvantaged groups. It is sad, but true, that terrible harms have been justified in the name of religion. The more important question is whether there is evidence that passage of the state's anti-discrimination law was motivated by religious animus, and unlike the situation in *Lukumi*, there is no evidence of that.

More concerning than the commissioner's statement was the fact that, on at least three other occasions, the state's Civil Rights Division had "considered the refusal of bakers to create cakes with images that conveyed disapproval of same-sex marriage, along with religious texts. Each time, the Division found that the baker acted lawfully in refusing service," on the grounds that the bakers felt the requested words and images were derogatory, hateful, or discriminatory. In these other cases the Division found no violation in part because "each bakery was willing to sell other products, including those depicting Christian themes, to the prospective customers," but in Phillips's case, his practice of selling other items to gay and lesbian customers was considered irrelevant. The Colorado court justified the differences in treatment by saying that the anti-gay messages were offensive while the requested message in Phillips's case was not, but Kennedy concluded that this "attempt to account for the difference in treatment elevates one view of what is offensive over another and itself sends a signal of official disapproval of Phillips' religious beliefs."

Our recommended approach agrees that the Court must take seriously the question of whether the state's seemingly neutral enforcement of its laws nevertheless reveals a hostility to religious practitioners. We think it was possible to distinguish the Phillips case from the other examples involving bakers; after all, no one in the litigation disputed that Phillips refused to bake a cake for Craig and Mullins because of their sexual orientation. As Justice Kagan wrote in her concurring opinion, "What makes the state agencies' consideration yet more disquieting is that a proper basis for distinguishing the cases was available—in fact was obvious." Colorado law "makes it unlawful for a place of public accommodation to deny 'the full and equal enjoyment' of goods and services to individuals based on certain characteristics, including sexual orientation and creed." The bakers in the other cases "did not violate that law" because they were asked to write messages "that they would not have made for any customer," thus treating the customers "in the same way they would have treated anyone else." By contrast, "the same-sex couple in this case requested a wedding cake that Phillips would have made for an opposite-sex couple," involving no special message or anything else distinguishing the cake from any other cake Phillips would have sold. This is what violated the state's requirement that customers receive "the full and equal enjoyment" of public accommodations regardless of their sexual orientation. "The different outcomes . . . could thus have been justified by a plain reading and neutral application of Colorado law—untainted by any bias against a religious belief."

Most important, though, we agree with Justice Kennedy that "the State's interest could have been weighed against Phillips' sincere religious objections in a way consistent with the requisite religious neutrality."[88] This means that there is no general right under the Free Exercise Clause for people engaged in the secular economy to be exempted from general anti-discrimination laws. It may be that, in cases involving individuals who are hired as artists or others engaged in personal expressive activity, there would be a right not to be forced to express oneself in a way that was contrary to their beliefs— for example, a custom cake baker may choose not to bake a cake that says "Hitler was right"—but that would implicate rights of free expression against compelled speech not general rights involving the free exercise of religion.[89] Also, nothing in the Colorado law would be violated if a baker refused to bake a cake on such grounds; the law prohibits only discrimination on the basis of race, sex, religion, and sexual orientation. If a vendor sells "Happy Birthday" cards, those cards must be sold to everyone, and the vendor cannot withhold the cards from members of a disfavored group because she or he is prejudiced against such people and does not personally want such people to have a happy birthday.

Justice Thomas, joined by Justice Gorsuch, concurred in part and concurred in the judgment, and argued that Masterpiece Cakeshop should prevail on its free speech claim: forcing it to design and bake a cake would be impermissible compelled expression. Subsequently, in August 2019, the Eighth Circuit, in *Telescope Media Group v. Lucero* ruled, 2–2–1, that it would be impermissible compelled speech to require a videographer take pictures at a same-sex wedding. The majority held that "even antidiscrimination laws, as critically important as they are, must yield to the Constitution," while the dissent pointed out that under the court's logic, "any time that a state's regulation of discriminatory conduct requires a person to provide services that 'express' something they dislike, the law is invalid."[90]

Although discussion of the speech issue is beyond our scope, we are very troubled by the implications of this argument. If designing and baking a cake, or taking pictures, are speech, then virtually any work can be deemed to have an expressive quality. This would create a basis for an exception to every civil rights law. Ollie's Barbecue could have justified refusing to serve African American customers on the ground that cooking and serving food is speech, and requiring service is impermissible compelled expression.[91] The Baptist owner of a printing business could refuse to print materials for a Mormon summer camp on the grounds that they consider Mormonism to be a cult rather than a legitimate religion. For both claims of free speech and free exercise of religion, courts should find a compelling government interest in stopping discrimination.

Unfortunately, there are reasons to worry that courts are becoming more accommodating of religious objectors who seek exemptions from anti-discrimination statutes. In *Brush & Nib Studios v. City of Phoenix* (2019), a bare majority of the Arizona Supreme Court held that Phoenix could not apply its Human Relations Ordinance to force the owners of a print shop to create custom wedding invitations celebrating same-sex wedding ceremonies in violation of their sincerely held religious beliefs. While "the Ordinance generally serves the compelling interest of ensuring equal access to publicly available goods and services," this "interest is not sufficiently overriding as to justify compelling Plaintiffs' speech by commandeering their creation of custom wedding invitations, each of which expresses a celebratory message, as the means of eradicating society of biases." The majority also held that "the Ordinance substantially burdens the free exercise of [the owners'] religious beliefs" and that the "purpose of eradicating discrimination . . . is not sufficiently overriding" to justify the substantial burden. Applying strict scrutiny, the majority concluded that creating an exemption for religious objectors would still allow the Ordinance to operate in most circumstances, and "it is not our role to speculate about whether exempting [these

THE FREE EXERCISE OF RELIGION

owners] would cause other businesses to seek a religious exemption from the Ordinance."

The dissenting justices argued that "our constitutions and laws do not entitle a business to discriminate among customers based on its owners' disapproval of certain religious groups, even if that disapproval is based on sincerely held religious beliefs." The dissenters noted that the Ordinance already exempted "bona fide religious organizations" that were not acting as part of a system of public accommodations, but insisted that commercial businesses serving the general public had to conform to such ordinances because the "fundamental object" of public accommodation laws is to prevent the "deprivation of personal dignity that surely accompanies denials of equal access to public establishments." The "'less restrictive means' contemplated by the majority—allowing businesses selectively to discriminate based on their owners' beliefs—enables the very conduct the Ordinance legitimately seeks to prohibit."

Writing separately in dissent, Justice Timmer argued that "in an ordered society of many beliefs, 'every person cannot be shielded from all the burdens incident to exercising every aspect of the right to practice religious beliefs,'" and when religious people choose to engage in commercial activities, "the limits they accept on their own conduct as a matter of conscience and faith are not to be superimposed on the statutory schemes which are binding on others in that activity."[92]

We agree. Attempting to manage the flood of circumstances where religious business owners seek exemptions from general laws will embroil courts in deeply divisive and politically fraught decisions about what is a religion, which religious claims are worth accommodating, why some religious practitioners and not others are exempted from general social duties, and why the value of granting an exemption is to be preferred over the social good associated with the law or regulation. This is why the Free Exercise Clause should be interpreted to prohibit government action that is motivated by animus toward particular religions or religious practitioners, or that targets religious beliefs, institutions, and practices, but should not provide a basis for exceptions from neutral laws of general applicability even if such laws impose burdens or inconveniences on religious people.

CONCLUSION

Ira Lupu and Robert Tuttle describe what they call "the mandatory regime of religious liberty," which is reflected in a set of key principles that are extremely well protected in American law. These include the right to worship as one chooses, the right to prepare and disseminate writings that contain materials for religious contemplation and worship, the right to proselytize to others about one's religious convictions, the right to be free of compulsion to worship in ways contrary to one's own beliefs, the right of parents to direct and control the religious upbringing of their children, and the right of religious sects to be treated equally with others under the law.[93] To this list we could add the right of religious institutions to select their clergy, control their doctrine, and determine how the organization is to be governed, without interference from the government.

The protection of these activities has been central to the freedom enjoyed by religious practitioners in the United States. The importance of this accomplishment should not be overlooked. As a result of these vitally important protections for religious liberty the United States is, by far, the most devout of all the Western democracies.[94] "Americans pray more often, are more likely to attend weekly religious services and ascribe higher importance to faith in their lives than adults in other wealthy, Western democracies, such as Canada, Australia, and most European states."[95] The Founders' vision of a secular government and a people free to exercise their religion has been realized.

This record of religious liberty is not tarnished if we decide not to mitigate all direct and indirect burdens on religious belief and conduct imposed by secular and neutral laws of general applicability. In free and diverse societies, it is enough if we are on guard against government action that is motivated by religious animus and if otherwise we seek merely to require everyone to play by the same rules. To do otherwise would be to place religious beliefs and behaviors in a privileged position next to the consciences and convictions of non-religious members of our community, and to entangle secular government officials in a no-win position of assessing all manner of religious beliefs and burdens against assertions of not-quite-compelling-enough government interests.

Still, we are concerned about the direction of the Supreme Court on these questions. In the October 2020 term the justices will consider the question of whether they should overturn the decision in *Employment Division v. Smith*. The case, *Fulton v. City of Philadelphia, Pennsylvania*, involves the question of whether the government can refuse to use a religious entity to place foster children if it refuses to do so with same-sex couples.[96] The justices accepted the case a year after four justices signaled that they would welcome an opportunity to take a fresh look at *Smith*, which (they claimed) "drastically cut back on the protection provided by the Free Exercise Clause."[97]

We have explained why we support the approach in *Smith* and would consider its overruling a mistake. We do not believe that people should be able to discriminate against others in the name of religion, or deny others medical care, or use religious beliefs as a basis for harming people by claiming a special status to be exempt from the same laws everyone else must follow. As Justice Ginsburg warned in *Hobby Lobby*, to enter this arena is to walk into a minefield. Not only should courts stay away from this minefield, but religious activists representing powerful mainstream religious entities risk eroding important secular democratic norms if they push to seek accommodations for their members in a way that denies access to otherwise available medical services and genuinely harms others who have fought long and hard to achieve some modest protections against discrimination in our civil law.

CHAPTER FIVE

Conclusion

Why Separation Is Not Hostility

IN THE 17TH century, most people in England believed that government should align itself closely with religious belief and conduct. It was a terrible and tumultuous time—repression, wars, rebellion—and people who sought to pray and worship in peace fled to other parts of the world, including the American colonies. The early colonists initially thought they would be most protected if they started colonies based on their own religious beliefs and practices and forced others to conform to their preferred established church. But over time, as the 18th century unfolded, the governing model of *establishment* (of an official religion) plus *conformity* (to government-approved religious doctrine and practice) was challenged by increasing numbers of people. A new idea emerged that envisioned a government that was separated from religious matters, one that was avowedly *secular* and *tolerant* of religious diversity. The goal was to get government out of the religion business.[1]

By the late 1780s this new idea had won the day in the former British colonies of North America. "Conflict over theology, liturgy, and church governance was confined to the private sector, the federal government was declared a permanent neutral, and all factions were given equal political rights and a guarantee of religious liberty no matter what faction took over the government."[2] Not everyone agreed, of course, and later Americans would continue to fight for greater government affiliation with religion. Moreover, unlike Revolutionary France, the United States did not attempt to secularize the larger political culture, and so there was no interest in the new republic in a thoroughly secular or rationalist public moral order. A different choice was made in the United States: in America, religious people should be able to be advocates for their religious beliefs and values in public. But the Constitution and the Bill of Rights constructed a government that claimed no relationship to any particular religion, insisted on no test for religious office, vested in the lawmaking body no authority to legislate on matters of religion, and specifically prohibited the passage of any law respecting an establishment of religion or prohibiting the free exercise thereof.

In previous chapters we have reviewed the major approaches to the Establishment and Free Exercise Clauses and the arguments for how they should be interpreted in our own time. We have explained why the concerns of the framers—which are even more powerful today in a far more religiously diverse society—should lead us to separate government as much as possible from associating itself with religious beliefs, practices, and symbols. In particular, we have emphasized that accommodationist approaches that increase government partnerships with particular religious practitioners risk increasing political conflict, inappropriate favoritism, the marginalization or exclusion of non-favored people, and political corruption of religious doctrine and practice. We think the evidence is clear: increased government affiliation with religion is a risk to our political system and to religion.

While we have addressed it in passing, there is one objection to our approach that deserves special attention. It is the claim—asserted repeatedly and vehemently by advocates of greater accommodation of religion—that our separationist position with regard to both the Establishment Clause and the Free Exercise Clause actually represents inappropriate hostility toward religious people and practices. When we say that government should not put up or continue to display monuments that are associated with particular religious traditions, they say that such a view reveals an unacceptable animosity to the religious heritage of the people and to the preferences of religious members of our community. When we say that government should not attempt to offer people with particular religious beliefs (but not others) exemptions from the social duties that are imposed on everyone else, they say that we are demonstrating a lack of respect for the conscience and convictions of religious people. Although we think we are advocating little more than reasonable separation and neutrality, they think such views are hostile to religion.

Depending on the justice and the period of time, one can hear the accusation of "hostility" in the Establishment Clause realm whenever one objects to (a) the government directly engaging in religious-like activities (e.g., opening government sessions with prayers or proclamations that reference God) that are couched as non-denominational and non-preferential, but actually reflect long-standing privileges given to some sects (e.g., Christian ministers) while excluding religious practices that have not been part of America's "history" or "traditions," (b) government officials who help organize certain types of religious practices but not others (e.g., working with Christian students to organize prayer sessions at school events), and (c) the government formally celebrating some religious traditions but not others (e.g., Christmas trees and creches, but not Islamic or Buddhist traditions and symbols).

In our view, objecting to these activities can only be considered hostile to religion if there is an assumption that the government should be allowed to align itself with Christian or Judeo-Christian practices and symbols because such symbols (and not other symbols) are part of our "traditions" and "heritage."[3] We reject that assumption as inconsistent with the Constitution's clear expectation that the government not formally align itself with particular religions.

When the Court declared that states could not pass laws requiring that public schools read from the Christian Bible at the opening of each school day, it was noteworthy that some objected on the grounds that ending government-sponsored prayer was itself hostile to religion. Writing for the Court in *Abington v. Schempp* (1963), Justice Clark disagreed that the only way to avoid being hostile to religion was to allow the government to engage in religious practices. "We agree of course that the State may not establish a 'religion of secularism' in the sense of affirmatively opposing or showing hostility to religion," but "we do not agree . . . that this decision in any sense has that effect. . . . [These] are religious exercises, required by the States in violation of the command of the First Amendment that the Government maintain strict neutrality, neither aiding nor opposing religion." He added:

> While the Free Exercise Clause clearly prohibits the use of state action to deny the rights of free exercise to anyone, it has never meant that a majority could use the machinery of the State to practice its beliefs. . . . The place of religion in our society is an exalted one, achieved through a long tradition of reliance on the home, the church and the inviolable citadel of the individual heart and mind. We have come to recognize through bitter experience that it is not within the power of government to invade

that citadel, whether its purpose or effect be to aid or oppose, to advance or retard. In the relationship between man and religion, the State is firmly committed to a position of neutrality.[4]

Similarly, when the Court in *Lynch v. Donnelly* (1984) concluded that it was all right for government to organize Christmas displays, including Nativity scenes, on government property, Justice Brennan explained on behalf of the four dissenters that "if government is to remain scrupulously neutral in matters of religious conscience, as our Constitution requires, then it must avoid those overly broad acknowledgments of religious practices that may imply governmental favoritism toward one set of religious beliefs."[5] It was this concern about government favoritism toward particular religions that led the Court to strike down the posting of the Ten Commandments in the schoolroom,[6] the prohibition on teaching principles of Darwinian evolution,[7] the requirement for mandatory Bible reading at the beginning of the school day,[8] mandatory reading of a government-composed prayer at public school,[9] and the use of public school facilities for religious instruction[10]—a pattern of government religious activity that was clearly tilted toward particular religious traditions that had a dominant place in the country's history and heritage.

We have no concerns when the government acknowledges religion in the course of engaging in secular activities. We also agree that there are certain references to God or deism that are acceptable because they are part of our heritage and take place in a context where they will not be mistaken for the government's engaging in the exercise of religion. We do not have to pretend that none of our leaders had religious sensibilities, and we do not have to write out of our history the Declaration of Independence or the Gettysburg Address. If such acknowledgments "have lost through rote repetition any significant religious content" then there is less reason to worry. There is a difference between having students memorize and recite the Gettysburg Address and having them read a prayer or set up a Nativity scene. Judges should focus on ensuring that the government's actions remain secular and neutral with respect to religion, rather than having them prohibit the government from making any mention whatsoever of religious matters.

We also agree that religious people in their private capacity should be free to declare their religious preferences through signs and symbols and should advocate their values. Nativity scenes on one's front lawn can fill the public sphere with piety just as does the lighting of Chanukah candles in one's home near the window or the wearing of a Hijab or an Amish bonnet or a Sikh turban or any other manner of non-governmental displays of religious pride or affiliation. Our position reveals no hostility toward religion. Our objection—and the Constitution's objection—is only to those who reference our history or traditions in order to justify government action that is inherently religious in nature. Like the framers of the Constitution, we want to secularize the government, not American society. We, like the framers, are hostile to government's engaging in religion, not to religion itself.

The rhetoric accusing those with our views of seeking to remove all religion from the public square is powerful, but disingenuous. It creates the false impression of seeking to cleanse religion from public life. But under our view of the First Amendment, religious observance and religious symbols do not belong in government activity or on government property; they are fully protected in the non-governmental realm. People can express their religious beliefs, wear and erect religious symbols, and even pray in public. In that sense, the charge of "cleansing religion from the public square" is inaccurate. But the government must be secular.

We acknowledge that even with this guidance there will be disagreements. Is "In God We Trust" on our money actually nothing more than a secular recognition of our heritage? Is the statement

"God Save This Honorable Court" before Supreme Court sessions a secular recognition rather than a religious activity? If the Pledge of Allegiance was changed in part because President Eisenhower listened to a Lincoln Day sermon that highlighted Lincoln's phrase "that this nation, under God, shall have a new birth of freedom," does that make it a secular acknowledgment or an essentially religious based activity? People will disagree and, indeed, the two of us disagree over some of these examples. But in our view, in working through these issues, the key imperative is maintaining the government's essentially secular nature and keeping it out of the business of religion. Also, we should keep in mind that just because a government action is constitutional, that does not make it desirable. We have a much better understanding now than our Founders had about how deistic invocations are exclusionary of the faith traditions of many of our fellow citizens, and it is always worth considering whether our practices can ensure that people of all faiths, and no faith, feel equally attached to our secular republic.

In opposing the use of "history" and "tradition" to justify government religious activity, we also seek to end the inherent hostility that such long-standing practices demonstrated toward historically excluded or disfavored religious traditions. Forcing schoolchildren to read from the Christian Bible is hostile toward students who do not share that faith tradition. Starting government sessions with prayers from only one religious tradition over a long period of time is hostile to members of the community who do not see their government embrace the practices or symbols of their faith. This would be obvious if a local township previously controlled by Christians came under the control of people affiliated with a different religion and started to offer different prayers at the beginning of their meetings.[11] The same with putting Nativity scenes or menorahs or the Ten Commandments on government property but not displays associated with Islam, the Baha'i, Rastafarianism, Buddhism, Hinduism,

Jainism, Sikhism, Taoism, Native American religions, Neopaganism, and hundreds of other traditions. These practices never had an opportunity to become part of our "traditions" or "heritage." In our view, expecting the government to be secular and neutral with respect to religion ends historic hostility toward most faith traditions and broadens toleration of the vast diversity of religious practitioners.

The hostility complaint against separation comes up in one other way in Establishment Clause cases, and that is with respect to the question of whether it is "hostile" to exclude religious institutions from receipt of government funds that might otherwise be available to non-religious institutions. Here the complaint starts with an assumption that "neutrality" is the baseline standard—one should treat religious institutions like any other institutions, and if one does not that is discriminatory and therefore hostile. But the constitutional requirement is not just that the government be neutral; it is that the government be neutral and secular. The government should do nothing that exhibits favoritism or hostility toward religion, but it must also refrain from participating in religious activities or providing material support to religious organizations. The government can do many things as a way of starting the day in a public school—have students sing the national anthem, listen to announcements—but it cannot start the school day with a prayer, even a silent prayer (although students can certainly start their day with a prayer at home, should they wish).[12] Similarly, the government can give money to entities for many purposes, but not for religious purposes, including capital improvements for church facilities. We understand that line-drawing may sometimes be difficult. Still, as long as disagreements take place within an assumption that aid must not implicate our secular government in religious activities, then the debates will proceed, in all their messiness, on the right track.

In the area of the Free Exercise Clause, one of the most prolific and well-respected scholar of religious liberty, Douglas Laycock,[13] starts with a proposition with which we agree: "The core point of religious liberty is that the government does not take positions on religious questions" including the question of whether religion is a good thing to be promoted or dangerous force to be contained. In our system religion was to be "confined to the private sector" and "the federal government was declared a permanent neutral." One goal of this plan was to minimize the bloody political consequences associated with government efforts to involve itself in religious matters; another was to "create a regime in which people of fundamentally different views about religion can live together in a peaceful and self-governing society." As Laycock notes, the framers understood that "beliefs about religion are often of extraordinary importance to the individual" but "beliefs at the heart of religion—beliefs about theology, liturgy, and church governance—are of little importance to the civil government." Consequently, it should be the case that "no religion can invoke the government's coercive power and no government can coerce any religious act or belief."

The difficulty arises when Professor Laycock extends the concept of religious act or belief to all "religiously motivated behavior."[14] This goes too far. Our view is that the Free Exercise Clause prohibits efforts to punish or discriminate against people for their religious beliefs, prohibits laws that target conduct associated with worship, and protects the right of religious institutions to select their clergy, control their doctrine, and determine how the organization is to be governed without government interference. If government is prohibited from passing any regulation that discourages any behavior that religious persons associate with their religious beliefs, then our secular political system would be obligated to treat religious people differently, and better, then everyone else. Religious people, and no one else, would be entitled to not conform their behavior to neutral and secular laws if they had a religious objection and if the government had no compelling reason to have them comply. They would be a law unto themselves. Government would be entangled in distinguishing religious from non-religious claims, or in determining whether a religious claim is serious or a mere pretext to receive the special benefit that religious people receive. This would be in contravention of Professor Laycock's "core point" that "government does not take positions on religious questions" and acts instead as "a permanent neutral."

Professor Laycock transforms a compelling case for the separation of government and religion into an argument that demands special accommodations for religious practitioners, and then claims that any refusal to extend these special accommodations reflects an inappropriate hostility to religious people. A reasonable requirement of neutrality becomes an unreasonable expectation of special treatment. He claims that "essential to the pursuit of religious neutrality" is that the law should offer special protections to the deeply held conscientious objections of religious people and some non-theists' deeply held convictions if they are "functionally equivalent" to religious views[15] (of the sort that the Court recognized in the Vietnam-era conscientious objector cases, *United States v. Seeger*[16] and *Welsh v. United States*[17]). However, "exemptions cannot be extended to political disagreement or personal needs whose only analogy to religion is that they may be deeply felt."[18] The refusal to provide special accommodations to religious objectors "pursues neutrality at the expense of liberty," resulting in a circumstance where "believers whose religion forbids compliance with certain laws would have to abandon religious behaviors of profound importance to them, or go to jail, or expatriate, or rebel against the government—even if the burdensome law serves no particularly important government interest."[19] In general, "Religion is different from other human activities, and the neutral course is to treat it differently."[20] As with the Establishment Clause versions of the hostility argument, any refusal to grant religion a special place in our formal legal and political practices is considered objectionable.

We can see the argument at work more clearly when we examine Professor Laycock's analysis of the rights of religious "wedding vendors" who are operating retail businesses that serve the general public but want nothing to do with same-sex weddings. Professor Laycock is distinctive among most strong advocates for religious liberty in that he supported a constitutional right to same-sex marriage.[21] But his view was conditioned on the Court's also recognizing the need to accommodate religious conscientious objectors. Under his view, if we legalize same-sex marriage over the objections of religious conservatives, it is only fair and balanced if we extend special exemptions to those who do not want to perform their social duties in relationship to that law. Professor Laycock recommends that "for very small businesses where the owner will be personally involved in providing any services, we should exempt marriage and relationship counselors, and we should exempt vendors from doing weddings or commitment ceremonies so long as another vendor is available without hardship to the same-sex couple." He views this as a matter of "reciprocal moral disapproval" between religious conservatives and gay rights advocates, and since religious conservatives must live with moral disapproval from the other side, the "desire of same-sex couples never to encounter such disapproval is not a sufficient reason to deprive others of religious liberty."[22]

Professor Laycock is concerned about the mutual hostility expressed between religious conservatives and supporters of gay rights, abortion rights, contraception, end of life matters—all the issues that heat up this corner of the culture wars. If the hostility is reciprocal, he believes the solution is for each side to show more respect for the other. He has urged both sides to work out deals and compromises at the state level, especially in red states that do not currently have public accommodation laws that prohibit private businesses from discriminating against people on the basis of sexual orientation. After all, the Supreme Court's decision on same-sex marriages binds only the government, not the private sector. He wants both sides to give a little.[23]

We have no objections to some politically arranged accommodations for conscientious objectors especially when they are most directly involved and genuinely complicit in deeply objectionable activities, such as the case of doctors or nurses who have personal moral objections to abortion (whether for religious reasons or otherwise). We also agree that religious organizations can hire on the basis of religion for positions where faith is essential to performing the task, such as for being a rabbi, a priest, or a minister.[24] This is recognized in state and federal law.[25] Members of the clergy do not have to perform religious services or rituals for any person they believe does not religiously qualify for those activities; for example, an orthodox rabbi may not consider a couple who follows Reform Jewish practices to be religious enough to have earned his participation in their ceremony. Not-for-profit religious organizations are typically exempted from state laws relating to same-sex marriage.[26] All of these reflect appropriate accommodations for religious liberty properly understood.

Beyond this, religious dissenters to government policy are no more entitled to feel that they are the victims of a hostile government than is any other dissenter. Selling flowers or cakes in public accommodations or providing health insurance to your secular employees is not an exercise of religion that government is obligated to accommodate. The concern of the framers was to prohibit the government from engaging in targeted religious animus; they were not worried about the possibility that religious people may be burdened in their everyday public activities by secular laws that advanced public interests and were motivated by no religious hostility. They expected religious people to comply with ordinary social duties—something easy to expect given that they separated the government from any authority to regulate on matters of religion.

It is no more hostile to require religious wedding vendors to follow the laws prohibiting discrimination against same-sex couples than it is to require religious apartment owners to rent to a gay man even if they believe God wants gay people to be shunned and isolated, or to require religious restaurant owners to serve blacks even if they believed God demanded separation of the races, or to require religious employers to hire women even if they believe that a woman's place is in the home, or to require religious retailers to allow regularly dressed women in their store even if they believe that women should be covered in public, or (for that matter) require gay business owners to serve religious conservatives even if they believe those conservatives perpetuate their vulnerable or marginalized position in American society.

Laws reflect hostility toward religion when they are motivated by animus toward certain religious practitioners. Laws do not reflect hostility toward religion merely because a secular government purpose is inconsistent with the beliefs of certain religious people. Slavery and Jim Crow were sustained for a long time by church teachings in certain parts of the country, but when civil rights laws were passed, those who disagreed were nevertheless expected to comply, and no hostility was assumed. The same with the second-class status of women in America as reflected in long-standing bans in employment, property ownership, even participation in ordinary civic functions such as juries. When those laws were changed to give women new freedoms and a new status in society, no one felt it was hostile to expect religious conservatives operating in public agencies or public accommodations to abide by the new law. A jury staff member in a local court might believe that a woman's place is in the home, but he was still expected to register women who responded to jury summonses. Religious dissenters had the liberty to publicly express their opposition to these developments, and they were free to engage in prayer and worship that urged God to help the country return to earlier ways. If they did so the government could not punish them; their religious views and practices would be protected. But in none of these earlier circumstances was it considered improperly hostile to expect compliance from dissenting religious practitioners. It is no different today.

It is likely that many laws burden many people's religious or moral sensibilities, even if they do not burden religious belief, worship, and the free exercise of religion. At the same time, the American people increasingly believe that women should have access to contraceptives and that public accommodations laws should be enforced. Throughout American history, the Supreme Court has refused to allow religious beliefs, practices, or sensibilities to justify the infliction of harm on others. That should continue to be the law.

We have defended ourselves against the accusation that our separationist positions reflect hostility to religion. But we end by making it clear that, in our view, separationist approaches to the interpretation of the Establishment and Free Exercises Clauses are the best way to protect and advance the extremely important value of religious freedom.

Preventing government officials from aligning themselves with certain religious practices and traditions ensures that the American republic will be a welcoming and supportive place for people of all faiths as well as for people of no particular religious faith. It also puts an end to the hostility that the government would otherwise exhibit toward non-favored religious practitioners. The country is made better when religious practitioners are free to proudly display their religious identities in public, and if they so choose on their own, to fill the public sphere with religious displays and symbols, so that we might celebrate people of faith and the great religious diversity of our fellow citizens. It would be wrong for anyone to attempt to rid the public discourse of all vestiges of religion. That would violate the rights of religious people, and it would improperly put the government in the position of preferring secular identities and cultures to religious ones. Principles of religious freedom and the separation of church and state, as well as freedom of speech, would prohibit such an effort.

In protecting the free exercise of religion, we decry efforts to act against religious people because of animus toward their religious views and practices. We insist that the government allow religious institutions to organize their own affairs to the largest extent possible. But we also remove the government from the impossible (and inevitably abused) challenge of deciding which religious people should be exempted from the social duties that are imposed on everyone else.

All of these principles add up to a tremendous amount of support for religion, even if they also mean an end to some traditionally favored religious sects having a special role in American law and politics.

Late in his life, when he was over 70 years of age, James Madison wrote a letter summarizing his views on the relationship between religion and politics. He wrote: "I have no doubt that every new example, will succeed, as every past one has done, in shewing [sic] that religion & Govt. will both exist in greater purity, the less they are mixed together."[27]

When the government is secular but also tolerant of the great diversity of religious traditions and practices, then the conditions exist for religion to thrive and for people to live in peaceful coexistence, subject only to the ordinary arguments about how best to advance the general welfare. In our view, there is nothing that threatens religion more than a government that itself attempts to be religious or that welcomes the efforts of more powerful religious sects to seek special treatment beyond the ordinary protections of their religious activities.

Current trends toward a greater mixing of government and religion are deeply disturbing. The Religious Clauses were the by-product of many hard lessons learned over many centuries, and we hope our discussion of them highlights both the mistakes that should be avoided and the most promising path forward.

Notes

. . .

1. The First Amendment, of course, says that "Congress" may not do this. In Everson v. Board of Education, 330 U.S. 1 (1947), the Court held that the Establishment Clause applies to state and local governments through its incorporation into the due process clause of the Fourteenth Amendment. It always has been assumed that the First Amendment applies to the president and to the federal courts, even though its text provides only a prohibition against "Congress."

2. *See*, e.g., American Legion v. American Humanist Association, 139 S.Ct 2067 (2019) (upholding 40-foot cross on government property).

3. *See*, e.g., Town of Greece v. Galloway, 572 U.S. 565 (2014) (upholding Christian prayers before town board meetings over a long period of time).

4. *See*, e.g., Mitchell v. Helms, 530 U.S. 793 (2000) (plurality opinion by Justice Thomas that the government may provide aid to parochial schools even if it is used for religious instruction).

5. 134 S. Ct. 2751 (2014).

6. *See* Masterpiece Cakeshop v. Colorado Civil Rights Commission, 138 S. Ct. 1819 (2018) (holding that the government violated the Free Exercise Clause when members of a civil rights commission articulated

"animus" against religion). *See also* Telescope Media Group v. Lucero, 936 F.3d 740 (8th Cir. 2019) (concluding that it violates freedom of speech under the First Amendment to hold a videographer liable under a state civil rights law for refusing to take videos at a same-sex wedding).

7. 137 S. Ct. 2012 (2017).

8. *Id.* at 2022.

9. 134 S. Ct. 1811 (2014).

10. 575 U.S. 682, 686 (2014).

11. 137 S. Ct. 2012 (2017).

12. 138 S. Ct. 2392 (2018).

13. Id. at 2433 (Sotomayor, J., dissenting).

14. 494 U.S. 872 (1990).

15. We, of course, acknowledge that sometimes the Court has interpreted the Free Exercise Clause to protect non-Christians as well. *See,* e.g., Gonzales v. O Centro Espirita Beneficente União do Veget, 546 U.S. 418 (2006) (holding that it violated the Religious Freedom Restoration Act to require an exception for a small religion that uses a hallucinogenic plant in making a tea); Church of the Lukumi Babalu Aye, Inc. v. Hialeah, 508 U.S. 520 (1993) (declaring unconstitutional a city ordinance that prohibited ritual sacrifice of animals because it was directed solely at a particular (non-Christian) religious sect).

16. See, for example, the Manhattan Declaration: A Call of Christian Conscience, the 2009 manifesto of conservative Christian principles set forth by Princeton professor Robert George and former Watergate conspirator Chuck Colson. Manhattan Declaration: A Call of Christian Conscience, Manhattan Declaration (Nov. 2009), http://manhattandeclaration.org/man_dec_resources/Manhattan_Declaration_full_text.pdf and List of Religious & Organizational Leaders Signatories, Manhattan Declaration, http://manhattandeclaration.org/man_dec_resources/list_of_religious_leaders.pdf.

17. See David Taylor, *"In God We Trust"—The Bills Christian Nationalists Hope Will "Protect Religious Freedom,"* THE GUARDIAN (Jan. 14, 2019), at https://www.theguardian.com/us-news/2019/jan/14/christian-nationalists-bills-religious-freedom-project-blitz (detailing efforts by the Christian right in America to introduce bills in American states).

NOTES

CHAPTER ONE

1. 134 S. Ct. 2751 (2014). The Religious Freedom Restoration Act is a federal law which provides that actions of the federal government must meet strict scrutiny. This is discussed in detail in Chapter 4 which addresses free exercise of religion.

2. *Id.* at 2785.

3. 134 S. Ct. 1811 (2014).

4. *Id.* at 1825.

5. 137 S. Ct. 2012 (2017).

6. *Id.* at 2022.

7. *Id.* at 2025.

8. 138 S. Ct. 1719 (2018).

9. Colo. Rev. Stat. §24-34-601(2)(a) (2017).

10. 138 S. Ct. at 1729.

11. 139 S.Ct. 2067 (2019).

12. *Id.* at 2074.

13. *Id.*

14. *Id.* at 2079.

15. In October Term 2019, the Court has a case which seems to pose this issue, Espinoza v. Montana Department of Revenue, 435 P.3d 603 (Mont. 2018), *cert. granted*, 139 S. Ct. 2777 (2019). The Montana Supreme Court ruled that it violated the Montana Constitution for the state to give tax credits that benefited religious schools. The Supreme Court has granted certiorari on the question of whether the denial of aid to religion violates the First Amendment.

16. *See* E. Digby Batzell, *The Protestant Establishment Revisited*, 45 THE AMERICAN SCHOLAR 499 (1976).

17. *See* Edward J. Larson, SUMMER FOR THE GODS: THE SCOPES TRIAL AND AMERICA'S CONTINUING DEBATE OVER SCIENCE AND RELIGION (2006).

18. Rory Carroll, *America's Dark and Not-Very-Distant History of Hating Catholics*, THE GUARDIAN (Sept., 12, 2015), at https://www.theguardian.com/world/2015/sep/12/america-history-of-hating-catholics and Maura Jane Farrelly, ANTI-CATHOLICISM IN AMERICA, 1620–1860 (2018).

19. J. Spencer Fluhman, "A PECULIAR PEOPLE": ANTI-MORMONISM AND THE MAKING OF RELIGION IN NINETEENTH-CENTURY AMERICA (2012).

20. Linda Gordon, THE SECOND COMING OF THE KKK: THE KU KLUX KLAN OF THE 1920S AND THE AMERICAN POLITICAL TRADITION (2017).

21. *See The Persecution of Jehovah's Witnesses: The Record of Violence against a Religious Organization Unparalleled in America since the Attacks on the Mormons*, American Civil Liberties Union (1941), available at http://debs.indstate.edu/a505p4_1941.pdf.

22. William G. McLoughlin, THE CHEROKEES AND CHRISTIANITY, 1794–1870: ESSAYS ON ACCULTURATION AND CULTURAL PERSISTENCE (Walter H. Conser, Jr. ed.) (2008).

23. Christopher L. Eisgruber & Lawrence G. Sager, RELIGIOUS FREEDOM AND THE CONSTITUTION (2007) at 2.

24. *See* John C. Jeffries, Jr., & James E. Ryan, *A Political History of the Establishment Clause*, 100 MICH. L. REV. 279, 283 (2001) (arguing that "Christian academies are energized by antipathy to the triumphant secularism of public education and by the desire to maintain or recreate in the private sphere the unselfconscious Protestant establishment that once dominated public life").

25. Tali Mendelberg, THE RACE CARD: CAMPAIGN STRATEGY, IMPLICIT MESSAGES, AND THE NORM OF RACIAL EQUALITY 85–86 (2001).

26. William Martin, WITH GOD ON OUR SIDE: THE RISE OF THE RELIGIOUS RIGHT IN AMERICA 171–72 (2000).

27. Quoted in S.I. Strong, *Christian Constitutions: Do They Protect Internationally Recognized Human Rights and Minimize the Potential for Violence Within a Society*, 29 CASE WESTERN RESERVE J. OF INT'L LAW 1, 2 (1997).

28. *Id.*

29. John C. Jeffries, Jr., & James Ryan, *A Political History of the Establishment Clause*, 100 MICH. L. REV. 279, 340 (2001).

30. Theocracy Watch, "The Rise of the Religious Right in the Republican Party," http://www.theocracywatch.org/taking_over.htm.

31. Robert Dreyfuss, *Reverend Doomsday: According to Tim LaHaye Apocalypse Is Now*, ROLLING STONE (Jan. 28, 2004).

32. Gary Wills, HEAD AND HEART: AMERICAN CHRISTIANITIES 490 (2007).

33. *Id.*

34. Ronald Reagan, Remarks to the National Association of Evangelicals (March 8, 1983), at 361. 1983 Pub. Papers 359, 361.

35. Ronald Reagan, Remarks at a White House Ceremony in Observation of National Day of Prayer (May 6, 1982), at 574.

36. *Id.*

NOTES

37. Ronald Reagan, Message to Congress Transmitting a Proposed Constitutional Amendment on Prayer in School (May 17, 1982).

38. *Id.*

39. David Crary, *Trump Steadily Fulfills Goals on Religious Right Wish List*, APNews (Aug. 20, 2019), at https://www.apnews.com/c8626c6bdbab4e3f8232ea1499a6954b.

40. Thomas Jefferson, Letter to Messrs. Nehemiah Dodge and others, a Committee of the Danbury Baptist Association, in Thomas Jefferson: Writings (Merrill D. Peterson ed., 1984) 510 (1802).

41. Lee v. Weisman, 505 U.S. 577, 640 (1992) (Scalia, J., dissenting)

42. Lee v. Weisman, 505 U.S. at 587 (1992).

43. 494 U.S. 872 (1990).

44. *Id.* at 878–89.

45. *Id.* at 879 (citation omitted).

46. *Id.* at 886–87.

47. United States v. Lee, 455 U.S. 252, 263fn2 (1982) (Stevens, J., concurring).

48. Sherbert v. Verner, 374 U.S. 398 (1963) (holding that it is a violation of the Free Exercise Clause to deny unemployment benefits to a woman who quit her job rather than work on her Saturday Sabbath).

49. As we discuss in Chapter 4, we disagree with the Court's conclusion that there was impermissible animus against religion in the Colorado Civil Rights Commission.

50. American Legion v. American Humanist Association, 139 S.Ct. 2067, 2095 (2019) (Thomas, J., concurring in the judgment): "The text and history of this Clause suggest that it should not be incorporated against the States. Even if the Clause expresses an individual right enforceable against the States, it is limited by its text to 'law[s]' enacted by a legislature, so it is unclear whether the Bladensburg Cross would implicate any incorporated right. And even if it did, this religious display does not involve the type of actual legal coercion that was a hallmark of historical establishments of religion. Therefore, the Cross is clearly constitutional."

51. *See*, e.g., Town of Greece v. Galloway, 572 U.S. at 610 (Thomas, J., concurring in the judgment) ("to the extent coercion is relevant to the Establishment Clause analysis, it is actual legal coercion that counts—not the 'subtle coercive pressures' allegedly felt by respondents in this case").

52. Lynch v. Donnelly, 465 U.S. 668, 694 (1984).
53. 139 S.Ct. 634 (2019)
54. *Id.* at 637.

1. Charles Carlton, CHARLES I, THE PERSONAL MONARCH, 2d ed., 65–70 (1995); Mark Charles Fissel, THE BISHOPS' WARS: CHARLES I's CAMPAIGNS AGAINST SCOTLAND, 1638–1640 (1994); Lawrence Kaplan, *Charles I's Flight to the Scots,* 11 ALBION 207–23 (1979); Anthony Gill, THE POLITICAL ORIGINS OF RELIGIOUS LIBERTY 2 (2007); James Hutson, RELIGION AND THE FOUNDING OF THE AMERICAN REPUBLIC 4 (1998); John Witte, Jr., & Joel A. Nichols, RELIGION AND THE AMERICAN CONSTITUTIONAL EXPERIMENT, 4th ed., 20 (2016); Michael Braddick, GOD'S FURY, ENGLAND'S FIRE: A NEW HISTORY OF THE ENGLISH CIVIL WARS (2008); C. V. Wedgwood, A KING CONDEMNED: THE TRIAL AND EXECUTION OF CHARLES I (1967); David Womersley, JAMES II: THE LAST CATHOLIC KING (2015).

2. The Act of Uniformity, 14 Car. II C. 4 (1662) and The Test Act, 25 Car. II C. 2 (1673); Roland Mushat Frye, *The Dissendence of Dissent and the Origins of Religious Freedom in America: John Milton and the Puritans,* 133 PROCEEDINGS OF THE AMERICAN PHILOSOPHICAL SOCIETY 475–88 (1989) and Sanford Kessler, *John Locke's Legacy of Religious Freedom,* 17 POLITY 484–503 (1985).

3. Nigel Aston, RELIGION AND REVOLUTION IN FRANCE, 1780–1804 (2000).

4. John K. Wilson, *Religion under the State Constitutions, 1776–1800,* 32 JOURNAL OF CHURCH AND STATE 753–73, 754 (1990).

5. 14 Car. II. C. 4 (1662); 25 Car. II C. 2.

6. Gill, THE POLITICAL ORIGINS OF RELIGIOUS LIBERTY, 2, 65.

7. Mark A. Graber & Howard Gillman, THE COMPLETE AMERICAN CONSTITUTIONALISM, VOLUME ONE: INTRODUCTION AND THE COLONIAL ERA, 324 (2015) and Gill, THE POLITICAL ORIGINS OF RELIGIOUS LIBERTY, 67–9.

8. Thomas J. Curry, THE FIRST FREEDOMS: CHURCH AND STATE IN AMERICA TO THE PASSAGE OF THE FIRST AMENDMENT 108–9 (1986).

9. Gill, THE POLITICAL ORIGINS OF RELIGIOUS LIBERTY, 95, 98, and William Penn, THE POLITICAL WRITINGS OF WILLIAM PENN 58 (2002); Witte and Nichols, RELIGION AND THE AMERICAN CONSTITUTIONAL EXPERIMENT, 21.

10. Gill, THE POLITICAL ORIGINS OF RELIGIOUS LIBERTY, 74, and Curry, THE FIRST FREEDOMS.

11. CHARTER OF RHODE ISLAND AND PROVIDENCE PLANTATIONS (1663), *reprinted in* THE COMPLETE BILL OF RIGHTS: THE DRAFTS, DEBATES, SOURCES, AND ORIGINS 34 (Neil H. Cogan ed., 1997); Perry Miller ed., THE COMPLETE WRITINGS OF ROGER WILLIAMS, 1:392 (1963).

12. Roger Williams, THE BLOUDY TENENT OF PERSECUTION FOR CAUSE OF CONSCIENCE 4 (Richard Groves ed., 2001) (1644). Note that "tenent" is an obsolete spelling of the word "tenet."

13. Thomas E. Buckley, CHURCH AND STATE IN REVOLUTIONARY VIRGINIA, 1776–1787, 3 (1977).

14. John Locke, A LETTER CONCERNING TOLERATION 34 (Patrick Romanell ed., 2d ed. Bobbs-Merrill 1955) (1689).

15. *English Historical Documents. Volume VIII, 1660–1714*, at 400 (A. Browning ed., 1953).; Gill, THE POLITICAL ORIGINS OF RELIGIOUS LIBERTY, 89.

16. Elisha Williams, THE ESSENTIAL RIGHTS AND LIBERTIES OF PROTESTANTS 7–8 (1744).

17. Charter of the Liberties and Frame of Government of Pennsylvania, art. XXXV (1682), ONLINE LIBRARY OF LIBERTY, available at https:// oll.libertyfund.org/pages/1682-charter-of-the-liberties-and-frame-of-government-of-pennsylvania; see also Ellis M. West, *The Right to Religious-Based Exemptions in Early America: The Case of Conscientious Objection to Conscription*, 10 JOURNAL OF LAW AND RELIGION 367–401 (1993/94); Benjamin Franklin, THE WORKS OF BENJAMIN FRANKLIN 3:78–80 (ed. Jared Sparks, rev. ed., 1840); Graber & Gillman, 1 COMPLETE AMERICAN CONSTITUTIONALISM at 343–44. For more on the contemporary debates, see Michael W. McConnell, *The Origins and Historical Understanding of Free Exercise of Religion*, 103 HARVARD LAW REVIEW 1409 (1990) and the response from Philip A. Hamburger, *A Constitutional Right of Religious Exemption: An Historical Perspective*, 60 GEORGE WASHINGTON LAW REVIEW 915, 916, 946 (1992) ("late nineteenth-century Americans tended to assume that the Free Exercise Clause did not provide a constitutional right to religious exemption from civil law" and "the

overwhelming majority of dissenters sought, not a constitutional right of exemption, but an end to establishments").

18. William Blackstone, BLACKSTONE'S COMMENTARIES ON THE LAWS OF ENGLAND 5:59 (ed. St. George Tucker, 1803) (1773).

19. Wilson, *Religion under State Constitutions*, 755.

20. *Id.* at 761.

21. N.Y. CONST. of 1777, art. XXXVIII, https://avalon.law.yale.edu/18th_century/ny01.asp#1; Mass. Const. of 1780, pt. I, art. III; Wilson, *Religion under State Constitutions*, 761–63.

22. Thomas Jefferson, NOTES ON THE STATE OF VIRGINIA, Query 17 (1832).

23. Thomas Buckley, CHURCH AND STATE IN REVOLUTIONARY VIRGINIA 108–9 (1977).

24. James Madison, *Memorial and Remonstrance against Religious Assessments, in* 2 THE WRITINGS OF JAMES MADISON 183 (Gaillard Hunt ed., 1900–1910) (1785).

25. Vincent Phillip Munoz, *James Madison's Principle of Religious Liberty*, 97 AM.POL.SCI.REV. 17–32, 21–24 (2003).

26. B. L. Rayner, SKETCHES OF THE LIFE, WRITINGS, AND OPINIONS OF THOMAS JEFFERSON 159–60 (1832).

27. John Leland, *The Rights of Conscience Inalienable*, in THE WRITINGS OF JOHN LELAND 179–92 (ed. L. F. Greene 1969) (1791).

28. Indeed, Justice Clarence Thomas, based on this, has said that the Establishment Clause should not be applied to state and local governments because it only was meant to keep the federal government from creating a national church that would interfere with state churches. *See*, e.g., Town of Greece v. Galloway, 572 U.S. 565, 604–8 (2014) (Thomas, J., concurring in part and concurring in the judgment); Elk Grove Unified School Dist. v. Newdow, 542 U.S. 1, 46 (2004) (Thomas, J., concurring in the judgment); Zelman v. Simmons-Harris, 536 U.S. 639, 679 (2002) (Thomas, J., concurring).

29. Wilson, *Religion under the States Constitutions*, 753 (1990) and Akhil Reed Amar, THE BILL OF RIGHTS: CREATION AND RECONSTRUCTION 32–33 (1998).

30. Oliver Ellsworth, A Landholder VII, CONNECTICUT COURANT (Dec. 17, 1787), reprinted in 14 THE DOCUMENTARY HISTORY OF THE CONSTITUTION 449–52 (J. Kaminski & G. Saladino eds. 1983); Joseph Story, COMMENTARIES ON THE CONSTITUTION § 1841 (1833).

31. The Debates in the Several State Conventions on the Adoption of the Federal Constitution, 4:118–9, 215 (J. Elliot, 2d ed., 1836).

32. See also Philip B. Kurland, *The Origins of the Religion Clauses of the Constitution*, 27 William and Mary L. Rev. 839, 848 (1986).

33. Howard Gillman, Mark A. Graber, & Keith E. Whittington, American Constitutionalism, Volume II: Rights and Liberties 99–100 (2d ed., 2017).

34. James Madison, The Papers of James Madison 12:201 (William T. Hutchinson ed., 1962–91), and 1 Annals of the Congress of the United States 452 (Joseph Gales ed., Gales and Seaton 1834) (1789–1791); Munoz, *James Madison's Principle of Religious Liberty*, 26.

35. Letter from George Washington, President of the United States, to the Hebrew Congregation in Newport, Rhode Island (August 18, 1790), available at https://www.tourosynagogue.org/history-learning/tsf-intro-menu/slom-scholarship/86-washington-letter.

36. Letter from Thomas Jefferson to a Committee of the Dansbury Baptist Association (Jan. 1, 1802), in Thomas Jefferson: Writings 510 (Merrill D. Peterson ed., 1984).

37. George Washington, Washington's Farewell Address to the People of the United States (Sept. 19, 1796). A recent study by Ellis M. West summarizes the 1790 consensus this way: "Most Americans understood the free exercise of religion to mean freedom from laws that take cognizance of religion, that is, laws that take a position for or against specific religions or religious doctrines and practices. This understanding of religious freedom also and necessarily means no laws discriminating on the basis of religion; it required equal treatment of all religions and of all persons regardless of their religion or lack thereof. Establishments of religion and laws characteristic of such establishments, therefore, were thought to violate the free exercise clause of religion, even if they impose no constraints on persons. Indeed, laws directly and intentionally aiding religion violate the free exercise of religion just as much as, if not more than, laws harming religion, or, perhaps better stated, laws aiding religion as such necessarily harm it." Ellis M. West, The Free Exercise of Religion in America: Its Original Constitutional Meaning, 196–97 (2019).

38. George Washington, Proclamation: A National Thanksgiving (Oct. 3, 1789), *reprinted in* 5 The Founders' Constitution, 94 (Philip B. Kurland

& Ralph Lerner eds., 2001); Letter from Thomas Jefferson to Levi Lincoln (Jan. 1, 1802), *reprinted in* 36 THE PAPERS OF THOMAS JEFFERSON, 256–57 (2009); Anson Phelps Stokes, 1 CHURCH AND STATE IN THE UNITED STATES 456 (1950).

39. Letter from Thomas Jefferson to Rev. Samuel Miller (Jan. 23, 1808), *in* THOMAS JEFFERSON: WRITINGS 1186–87 (Merrill D. Peterson, ed., 1984); Letter from Thomas Jefferson to Messrs. Nehemiah Dodge, Ephraim Robbins, and Steven S. Nelson, a Committee of the Danbury Baptist Association in the State of Connecticut (Jan. 1, 1802) (in Library of Congress, microfilm); Hamburger, *A Constitutional Right of Religious Exemption*, 928; Kurt T. Lash, *Second Adoption of Free Exercise Clause: Religious Exemptions under the Fourteenth Amendment*, 88 Nw. U. L. REV. 1106, 1145 (1994); Cong. Globe, 38th Cong., 1st Sess. 208 (1864).

40. *See* Church of Holy Trinity v. United States, 143 U.S. 457, 471 (1892) (Brewer, J.) ("this is a Christian nation").

41. Van Orden v. Perry, 545 U.S. 677, 731 (Stevens, J., dissenting).

CHAPTER THREE

1. Van Orden v. Perry, 545 U.S. 677, 681 (2005).

2. See, e.g., Linda Greenhouse, *The Ten Commandments Reach the Supreme Court*, N.Y. TIMES (Feb. 28, 2005), at A12; Sylvia Moreno, *Supreme Court on a Shoestring: Homeless Man Takes on Texas Religious Display*, WASH. POST (Feb. 21, 2005), at A1.

3. Jeffrey Gettleman, *Monument Is Now Out of Sight, but Not Out of Mind*, N.Y. TIMES (Aug. 28, 2003), at A14; see also Moore v. Judicial Inquiry Comm'n, 891 So. 2d 848, 862 (Ala. 2004).

4. Glassroth v. Moore, 242 F. Supp. 2d 1068, 1068 (M.D. Ala. 2003); see also Shaila K. Dewan, *The Big Name in Alabama's Primary Isn't on the Ballot*, N.Y. TIMES (May 30, 2004), at N16.

5. Rachel Chason, *A Short History of Roy Moore's Controversial Interpretations of the Bible*, WASH. POST (Sept. 27, 2017), https://www.washingtonpost.com/news/acts-of-faith/wp/2017/09/27/a-short-history-of-roy-moores-controversial-interpretations-of-the-bible/. The same story quotes Moore as expressing the view that Islam is a false religion and

that Muslims should not be allowed to serve in Congress. *See also* Roy
Moore, So Help Me God: The Ten Commandments, Judicial Tyranny,
and the Battle for Religious Freedom (2005).

6. Cleve R. Wootson, Jr., *Why One Man Keeps Ramming His Car into
Ten Commandments Statutes on Government Property*, Wash. Post (June 28,
2017), https://www.washingtonpost.com/news/acts-of-faith/wp/2017/06/28/
why-one-man-keeps-ramming-his-car-into-ten-commandments-statues-

7. Thomas Jefferson, Letter to Messrs. Nehemiah Dodge and
others, a Committee of the Danbury Baptist Association, in Thomas
Jefferson: Writings (Merrill D. Peterson ed., 1984) 510 (1802).

8. 330 U.S. 1, 18 (1947).

9. *Id.* at 14 (Jackson, J., dissenting).

10. *Id.* at 31–32.

11. *See* Alan Schwarz, *No Imposition of Religion: The Establishment
Clause Value*, 77 Yale L.J. 692, 708 (1968).

12. Justice Brennan has articulated these purposes behind the

> The first, which is most closely related to the more general concep-
> tions of liberty found in the remainder of the First Amendment,
> is to guarantee the individual right to conscience. . . . The second
> purpose of separation and neutrality is to keep the state from inter-
> fering in the essential autonomy of religious life, either by taking
> upon itself the decision of religious issues, or by unduly involving
> itself in the supervision of religious institutions or officials. The
> third purpose of separation and neutrality is to prevent the triviali-
> zation and degradation of religion by too close an attachment to the
> organs of government. . . . Finally, the principles of separation and
> neutrality help assure that essentially religious issues, precisely be-
> cause of their importance and sensitivity, not become the occasion
> for battle in the political arena.

Marsh v. Chambers, 463 U.S. 783, 803–5 (1983) (Brennan, J., dissenting)

13. Professor Lupu has argued that strict separation was the dominant
theory for the Establishment Clause from 1947 to 1980, but that since then

its role in Supreme Court decisions has greatly waned. Ira C. Lupu, *The Lingering Death of Separationism*, 62 GEO. WASH. L. REV. 230 (1994).

14. Philip Kurland, *Of Church and State and the Supreme Court*, 29 U. CHI. L. REV. 1, 96 (1961).

15. Douglas Laycock, *Formal, Substantive, and Disaggregated Neutrality toward Religion*, 39 DEPAUL L. REV. 993, 1001 (1990).

16. Lynch v. Donnelly, 465 U.S. 668, 694 (1984).

17. County of Allegheny v. American Civil Liberties Union, Greater Pittsburgh Chapter, 492 U.S. 573, 627 (1989) (O'Connor, J., concurring in part and concurring in the judgment) (citations omitted).

18. For a prescient prediction of the development of the symbolic endorsement test and a description of its ambiguity, see William P. Marshall, *"We Know It When We See It," the Supreme Court and Establishment*, 59 S. CAL. L. REV. 495 (1986).

19. 515 U.S. 753 (1995).

20. Justice Scalia—writing for a plurality of Rehnquist, Kennedy, and Thomas—rejected the symbolic endorsement test. He said that the symbolic endorsement approach "exiles private religious speech to a realm of less-protected expression. . . . [T]he Establishment Clause . . . was never meant to serve as an impediment to purely private religious speech connected to the State only through its occurrence in a public forum." *Id.* at 766–67.

21. *Id.* at 777 (O'Connor, J., concurring in the judgment).

22. *Id.* at 776

23. *Id.* at 780.

24. *Id.* at 780–81.

25. *Id.* at 799–800 (Stevens, J., dissenting).

26. *Id.* at 800 n.5.

27. For a defense of the symbolic endorsement test, *see* Jesse Choper, SECURING RELIGIOUS LIBERTY: PRINCIPLES FOR JUDICIAL INTERPRETATION OF THE RELIGION CLAUSES 28–29 (1995); Arnold H. Loewy, *Rethinking Government Neutrality towards Religion under the Establishment Clause: The Untapped Potential of Justice O'Connor's Insight*, 64 N.C. L. REV. 1049 (1986).

28. *See*, e.g., Marshall, *supra* note 19, at 537; Steven D. Smith, *Symbols, Perceptions, and Doctrinal Illusions: Establishment Neutrality and the "No Endorsement" Test*, 86 MICH. L. REV. 266, 283 (1987) (identifying this and other problems with the symbolic endorsement test).

29. Allegheny County v. Greater Pittsburgh ACLU, 492 U.S. at 674.

30. Lee v. Weisman, 505 U.S. 577, 587 (1992).

31. Allegheny County v. Greater Pittsburgh ACLU, 492 U.S. at 660 (Kennedy, J., concurring in the judgment in part and dissenting in part).

32. *See*, e.g., Mitchell v. Helms, 530 U.S. 793 (2000). Justice Thomas refers to this as the government being neutral in its treatment of religion. To avoid confusion with the "neutrality theory" described earlier, this is described here as requiring equal treatment for religious and nonreligious groups and activities.

33. 505 U.S. 577 (1992).

34. *Id*. at 604 (Blackmun, J., concurring).

35. *Id*. at 640 (Scalia, J., dissenting).

36. 572 U.S. 565, 610 (2014) (Thomas, J., concurring in the judgment).

37. Michael W. McConnell, *Accommodation of Religion*, 1985 Sup. Ct. Rev. 1, 14.

38. Professor Sherry argues that the coercion test "makes the Establishment Clause redundant. Any government action that coerces religious belief violates the Free Exercise Clause." Suzanna Sherry, Lee v. Weisman: *Paradox Redux*, 1992 Sup. Ct. Rev. 123, 134.

39. Allegheny County v. Greater Pittsburgh ACLU, 492 U.S. at 627–8 (O'Connor, J., concurring in part and concurring in the judgment).

40. 492 U.S. 573 (1989).

41. *Id*. at 650.

42. *Id*. at 679 (Kennedy, J., concurring in the judgment in part and dissenting in part).

43. *Id*. at 637 (O'Connor, J., concurring and concurring in the judgment).

44. 545 U.S. 677 (2005).

45. 139 S.Ct. 2067 (2019).

46. *Id*. at 2074.

47. *Id*. at 2075.

48. *Id*. at 2095 (Thomas, J., concurring in the judgment).

49. *Id*. at 2098 (Gorsuch, J., concurring in the judgment).

50. *Id*.

51. *Id*. at 2092 (Kavanaugh, J., concurring).

52. *Id*. at 2093.

53. Justices Breyer and Kagan each wrote concurring opinions about why the cross did not violate Establishment Clause principles, though

neither indicated support for an accommodationist approach to that provision.

54. *Id.* at 2105 (Ginsburg, J., dissenting).

55. *See,* e.g., Eric J. Segall, Originalism as Faith (2018).

56. Youngstown Sheet & Tube Co. v. Sawyer, 343 U.S. 579, 634 (1952) (Jackson, J., concurring) (discussing the intended scope of the executive power).

57. Abington School Dist. v. Schempp, 374 U.S. at 237.

58. Wallace v. Jaffree, 472 U.S. 38, 113 (1985) (Rehnquist, J., dissenting).

59. 515 U.S. 819, 854–8 (1995) (Thomas, J., concurring); *id.* at 868–73 (Souter, J., dissenting). James Madison issued his famous Remonstrance in arguing against a Virginia decision to renew a tax to support the church. This is reviewed in detail in *Everson v. Board of Education,* 330 U.S. 1, 12 (1947); *id.* at 31–34 (Rutledge, J., dissenting).

60. Laurence H. Tribe, AMERICAN CONSTITUTIONAL LAW 1158–1160 (2d ed. 1988).

61. *Id.* at 1158–1559 (citations omitted).

62. James Madison, Federalist No. 51, THE FEDERALIST PAPERS 322 (C. Rossiter ed. 1961).

63. Abington School Dist. v. Schempp, 374 U.S. at 240 (Brennan, J., concurring).

64. *See* Justin Driver, THE SCHOOLHOUSE GATE: PUBLIC EDUCATION, AND THE BATTLE FOR THE AMERICAN MIND (2018) (discussing changes in public education and constitutional issues, including concerning religion in the schools).

65. *Id.* at 238.

66. Reynolds v. United States, 98 U.S. 145, 164 (1878) (quoting Jefferson's letter to the Danbury Baptist Association). This was the first reference in the Supreme Court to "Jefferson's now ubiquitous . . . statement." Mark J. Chadsey, *Thomas Jefferson and the Establishment Clause,* 40 AKRON L. REV. 623, 638 n.67 (2007).

67. Everson, 330 U.S. at 18.

68. *Id.* at 15; *id.* at 31–32 (Rutledge, J., dissenting); see also Lee v. Weisman, 505 U.S. 577, 600–01 (1992) (Blackmun, J., concurring) (discussing the agreement between the majority and dissent in *Everson* with Jefferson's conception of strict separation).

69. Lynch v. Donnelly, 465 U.S. 668, 688 (1984) (O'Connor, J., concurring).

70. See James Madison, Memorial and Remonstrance against Religious Assessment (June 20, 1785), in 8 THE PAPERS OF JAMES MADISON 295, 298–306 (Robert A. Rutland et al. eds., 1973) (urging the Commonwealth of Virginia not to enact a bill providing support to religious groups through the levy of a tax).

71. See, e.g., Henry Kamen, THE SPANISH INQUISITION: AN HISTORICAL REVISION 10–11 (1997) (discussing the status of conversos—Jews or Muslims who had been forced to convert to Christianity—and the continuing pressure to conform in 14th-century Spain).

72. 370 U.S. at 431.

73. See, e.g., Lee v. Weisman, 505 U.S. 577 (1992) (holding that the Establishment Clause forbids prayer at public school graduations); Wallace v. Jaffree, 472 U.S. 38 (1985) (striking down a statute authorizing "moments of silence" at public schools as violating the Establishment Clause); Sch. Dist. of Abington Twp. v. Schempp, 374 U.S. 203 (1963) (finding that the Establishment Clause barred reading Bible passages in public schools); Engle v. Vitale, 370 U.S. 421 (1962) (holding that states may not compose official prayer to be read in public schools).

74. Josh White, *Intolerance Found at Air Force Academy*, WASH. POST (June 23, 2005), at A2.

75. See James P. Byrd, Jr., THE CHALLENGES OF ROGER WILLIAMS 121–27 (2002) ("In the process of corrupting the church, Williams believed that Christendom had corrupted biblical exegesis by devising an interpretative method that supported the state's claim to authority over religious matters").

76. We develop this point more fully in Chapter 5.

77. 370 U.S. 421 (1962).

78. *Id.* at 422.

79. *Id.* at 430.

80. *Id.* at 431–2.

81. *Id.* at 435.

82. 374 U.S. 203 (1963).

83. *Id.* at 225.

84. 472 U.S. 38 (1985).

85. Justice Powell noted in his concurring opinion that "the record before us . . . makes clear that Alabama's purpose was solely religious in character." *Id.* at 65 (Powell, J., concurring).

86. *Id.* at 56.

87. 505 U.S. 577 (1992).

88. *Id.* at 586–7.

89. *Id.* at 592.

90. *Id.* at 604, 606 (Blackmun, J., concurring).

91. *Id.* at 638.

92. *Id.* at 645.

93. 530 U.S. 290 (2000).

94. *Id.* at 302.

95. *Id.* at 307.

96. *Id.* at 312 (citations omitted).

97. *Id.* at 318 (Rehnquist, C.J., dissenting).

98. The one situation where prayer would be permissible would be if it were conducted by students as part of a non-curricular use of school facilities. The Supreme Court has held that government may not exclude student religious groups from using school facilities on the same terms as non-religious groups (Widmar v. Vincent, 454 U.S. 263 [1981]) and has upheld the federal Equal Access Act that prohibits schools that are receiving federal funds from discriminating against student groups in access to facilities based on their religious or philosophical activities or beliefs. Board of Educ. of Westside Community Schools v. Mergens, 496 U.S. 226 (1990).

99. *See* Paul G. Kauper, Prayer, *Public Schools and the Supreme Court*, 61 MICH. L. REV. 1031, 1046 (1963) ("immature and impressionable children are susceptible to a pressure to conform and to participate in the expression of religious beliefs that carry the sanction and compulsion of the state's authority").

100. Erwin Griswold, *Absolute Is in the Dark: A Discussion of the Approach of the Supreme Court to Constitutional Questions*, 8 UTAH L. REV. 167, 177 (1963).

101. 463 U.S. 783 (1983).

102. *Id.* at 786.

103. *Id.* at 791.

104. *Id.* at 792–3.

105. *See id.* at 797 (Brennan, J., dissenting) ("That the 'purpose' of legislative prayer is preeminently religious rather than secular seems to me to be self-evident").

106. *Id.* at 798–99.

107. 134 S. Ct. 1811 (2014).

108. *Id.* at 1819.

109. *Id.* at 1822.

110. *Id.* at 1825. Justice Thomas wrote an opinion concurring in part and concurring in the judgment, which was joined in part by Justice Scalia. Writing for just himself, Justice Thomas reiterated his view that the Establishment Clause does not apply to state and local governments; it was, in his view, meant only to keep Congress from creating a national church that could rival state churches. *Id.* at 1835. In a part of the opinion joined by Justice Scalia, Justice Thomas argued that the Establishment Clause is violated only if there is "actual legal coercion" to participate in religious activities. *Id.* at 1838.

111. Justice Breyer also wrote a dissenting opinion and stated: "The town of Greece failed to make reasonable efforts to include prayer givers of minority faiths, with the result that, although it is a community of several faiths, its prayer givers were almost exclusively persons of a single faith. Under these circumstances, I would affirm the judgment of the Court of Appeals that Greece's prayer practice violated the Establishment Clause." *Id.* at 1841 (Breyer, J., dissenting).

112. *Id.* at 1841 (Kagan, J., dissenting).

113. *Id.* at 1841–1842 (Kagan, J., dissenting).

114. 465 U.S. 668 (1984).

115. *Id.* at 681.

116. *Id.* at 711 (Brennan, J., dissenting).

117. 492 U.S. 573 (1989).

118. 515 U.S. 753 (1995).

119. 139 S.Ct. 2067 (2019).

120. Id. at 2107 (Ginsburg, J., dissenting).

121. Madison's Remonstrance is reprinted in Everson v. Board of Educ., 330 U.S. 1, 63 (1947).

122. *See*, e.g., Lemon v. Kurtzman, 403 U.S. at 614 ("Fire inspections, building and zoning regulations, and state requirements under compulsory school attendance laws are examples of necessary and permissible contacts").

123. In the initial case concerning government aid to parochial schools, Everson v. Board of Education, 330 U.S. 1 (1947), the Court upheld the constitutionality of the government's reimbursing parents for the costs of bus transportation to and from parochial school. The Court recognized that "there is even a possibility that some of the children might not be sent to the church schools if the parents were compelled . . . to pay their children's bus fares out of their own pockets . . . when transportation to a public school would have been paid for by the State." *Id.* at 17.

124. 403 U.S. 602 (1971).

125. Everson v. Board of Educ., 330 U.S. 1 (1947).

126. Wolman v. Walter, 433 U.S. 229 (1977).

127. Committee for Pub. Educ. and Religious Liberty v. Regan, 444 U.S. 646 (1980).

128. Levitt v. Committee for Pub. Educ., 413 U.S. 472 (1973).

129. 530 U.S. 793 (2000). For competing views of the equality theory the Court follows in *Mitchell, see* Alan E. Brownstein, *Interpreting the Religion Clauses in Terms of Liberty, Equality, and Free Speech Values—A Critical Analysis of "Neutrality Theory" and Charitable Choice*, 13 *Notre Dame J.L. Ethics & Pub. Pol'y.* 243 (1999) (criticizing equality theory); Michael W. McConnell, *State Action and the Supreme Court's Emerging Consensus on the Line between Establishment and Private Religious Expression*, 28 Pepp. L. Rev. 681 (2001) (defending equality approach).

130. 530 U.S. at 809.

131. *Id.*

132. *Id.* at 828.

133. *Id.*

134. *Id.* at 839–40 (O'Connor, J., concurring in the judgment).

135. *Id.* at 840–41.

136. *Id.* at 868.

137. *Id.* at 868–69.

138. *Id.* at 913.

139. 137 S. Ct. 2012 (2017). Although this case involved the Free Exercise Clause, which we discuss in the next chapter, since it involves government aid to religion it is discussed here with cases concerning that topic.

140. *Id.* at 2022.

141. *Id.* at 2025.

142. *Id.* at 2027 (Sotomayor, J., dissenting).

143. *Id.* at 2024 n.3.

144. 137 S.Ct. at 2017.

145. *Id.* at 2021.

146. *Id.* at 2022.

147. 540 U.S. 712 (2004).

148. Washington Constitution, Art. I, §11.

149. 474 U.S. 481 (1986).

150. Locke v. Davey, 540 U.S. at 718.

151. *Id.* at 719.

152. *Id.* at 726 (Scalia, J., dissenting).

153. Locke v. Davey, 540 U.S. at 725.

154. 137 S.Ct. at 2023.

155. *Id.*

156. *See,* e.g., Michele Estrin Gilman, *"Charitable Choice" and the Accountability Challenge: Reconciling the Need for Regulation with the First Amendment Religion Clauses,* 55 VAND. L. REV. 799 (2002); Andrea Pallios, *Should We Have Faith in the Faith-Based Initiative: A Constitutional Analysis of President Bush's Charitable Choice Plan,* 30 HASTINGS CONST. L.Q. 131 (2002); David J. Freedman, *Wielding the Ax of Neutrality: The Constitutional Status of Charitable Choice in the Wake of* Mitchell v. Helms, 35 U. RICH. L. REV. 313 (2001); Alan E. Brownstein, *Interpreting the Religion Clauses in Terms of Liberty, Equality, and Free Speech Values—A Critical Analysis of "Neutrality Theory" and Charitable Choice,* 13 NOTRE DAME J. L. ETHICS & PUB. POL'Y 243 (1999).

157. 137 S.Ct. at 2028-29 (Sotomayor dissenting).

158. *Id.* at 2038.

159. 393 Mont. 446 (2018), *cert. granted,* 139 S. Ct. 2777 (June 28, 2019) (No. 18-1195)..

160. *See* Lemon v. Kurtzman, 403 U.S. 602, 612–13 (1971).

161. *See* Trinity Lutheran Church of Columbia, Inc. v. Comer, 137 S. Ct. 2012, 2024 n.3 (2017).

162. Locke v. Davey, 540 U.S. 712, 723 (2004).

163. McCreary County, Ky. v. American Civil Liberties Union of Ky., 545 U.S. 844, 882 (2005) (O'Connor, J., dissenting).

CHAPTER FOUR

1. See Erwin Chemerinsky and Michele Goodwin, *Religion Is Not a Basis for Harming Others: Review Essay of Paul A. Offit's Bad Faith: When Religious Belief Undermines Modern Medicine*, 104 Geo. L. J. 1111 (2016), 1111–12; Ann M. Simmons, *How a County Clerk Is Refusing to Issue Gay Marriage Licenses and Defying the Supreme Court*, L.A. TIMES (Aug. 18, 2015), http://www.latimes.com/nation/nationnow/la-na-nn-kentucky-marriage-license-20150818-htmlstory.html; Elane Photography, LLC v. Willock, 309 P.3d 53, 77 (N.M. 2013) (holding that a photographer could not refuse to take pictures at a same-sex wedding based on religious beliefs); Burwell v. Hobby Lobby Stores, Inc., 134 S. Ct. 2751, 2759 (2014) (holding that the contraceptive requirement, as applied to closely held corporations, violated the Religious Freedom Restoration Act of 1993 (RFRA), 42 U.S.C. § 2000bb [2000]); Stormans, Inc. v. Wiesman, 794 F.3d 1064, 1071 (9th Cir. 2015) (holding that a regulation requiring pharmacies to timely deliver all prescription medications, even if the pharmacy owner had a religious objection, was facially neutral for purposes of the Free Exercise Clause and constitutional).

2. 98 U.S. 145 (1879).

3. Martha M. Ertman, *The Story of* Reynolds v. United States: *Federal "Hell Hounds" Punishing Mormon Treason*, in Family Law Stories 68–69 (Carol Sanger ed., 2008); 37th US Congress, Sess. 2, ch.126, 12 Stat. 501.

4. 98 U.S. 145, 164, 166–67.

5. See Kurt T. Lash, *The Second Adoption of the Free Exercise Clause: Religious Exemptions under the Fourteenth Amendment*, 88 Nw. U. L. Rev. 1106, 1115; Letter from Thomas Jefferson to Rev. Samuel Miller (Jan. 23, 1808), in Thomas Jefferson: Writings (Merrill D. Peterson ed., 1984), 1186; Letter from Thomas Jefferson to a Committee of the Danbury Baptist Association (Jan. 1, 1802), in Thomas Jefferson: Writings (Merrill D. Peterson ed., 1984), 510. This refusal to exempt religious practitioners from general social duties was commonplace in the 19th century. See Lash, *Second Adoption of Free Exercise Clause*, 1122 (1994) ("religious exemptions were regularly denied") and the citations in the accompanying footnote.

6. Davis v. Beason, 133 U.S. 333, 341–45 (1890).

7. 321 U.S. 158, 168 (1944).

8. People v. Pierson, 68 N.E. 243, 246 (N.Y. 1903).

9. 366 U.S. 599, 603–4, 606–7, 613–14 (1961) (emphasis added).

10. 374 U.S. 398, 403, 407, 412 (1963).

11. See Thomas v. Review Bd., 450 U.S. 707 (1981) (holding that denying unemployment benefits to a Jehovah's Witness who left his job because his religious beliefs forbade him from fulfilling his duties "constituted a violation of his First Amendment right to free exercise of religion").

12. 406 U.S. 205, 216, 218, 222, 235, 241, 245–46 (1972).

13. See, e.g., Larson v. Valente, 456 U.S. 228 (1982) (government discrimination among religions must meet strict scrutiny).

14. 406 U.S. 205 at 246.

15. See Chemerinsky and Goodwin, *Religion Is Not a Basis for Harming Others*, 1119.

16. 455 U.S. 252, 257–60, 263fn2 (1982).

17. 461 U.S. 574 (1983).

18. 475 U.S. 503 (1986).

19. 482 U.S. 342 (1987).

20. 476 U.S. 693 (1986). Later scholarly analysis of the justices' internal deliberations in *Bowen v. Roy* reveal the justices' concern with a possible slippery slope if religious believers were exempt from generally applicable laws and regulations. The papers also highlight internal battles on the Court over the difference between having the government use already existing social security numbers and requiring religious objectors to provide numbers for young children. See Paul E. McGreal, *The Making of the Supreme Court's Free Exercise Clause Jurisprudence: Lessons from the Blackmun and Powell Papers in* Bowen v. Roy, 34 S. ILL. U. J.L. 469 (2010).

21. 485 U.S. 439, 442, 448, 450–52, 457–58, 468, 476 (1988).

22. See Peter Zwick, *Redeemable Loss: Lyng, Lower Courts and American Indian Free Exercise on Public Lands*, 60 CASE W. RES. L. REV. 241, 243 (2009) (noting the failure "to appreciate the grave importance of specific sites to Indian religions because site-specificity is not an essential concept in conventional Western religious thought").

23. 494 U.S. 872, 875, 878–80, 886–89, 890, 893–94, 902, 918–19 (1990) (internal citations omitted).

24. 42 U.S.C. § 2000bb-1(a)-(b) (2012).

25. 521 U.S. 507, 519 (1997).

26. 42 U.S.C. § 2000cc (2012).

27. Ira C. Lupu, Hobby Lobby *and the Dubious Enterprise of Religious Exemptions*, 38 HARV. J.L. & GENDER 35, 68 & n.156 (2015); Christopher

C. Lund, *Religious Liberty after* Gonzales: *A Look at State RFRAs*, 55 S.D.
L. Rev. 466, 467 (2010).

28. 546 U.S. 418 (2006).

29. 134 S. Ct. 2751 (2014).

30. One quantitative study concludes that plaintiffs in strict scrutiny
cases usually win only if they can also show that a law was either non-
neutral or not of general applicability, thus further blurring the practical
differences between the approaches taken in *Yoder* and *Smith*. See Caleb
C. Wolanek and Heidi Liu, *Applying Strict Scrutiny: An Empirical Analysis
of Free Exercise Cases*, 78 Mont. L. Rev (2017).

31. 508 U.S. 520, 526, 534, 538 (1993).

32. Trump v. Hawaii, 138 S. Ct. 2392, 2433 (2018) (Sotomayor, J.,
dissenting) (criticizing the majority's decision to uphold the president's
"travel ban" restrictions on entry to the United States by nationals from certain foreign countries on the grounds that the decision "leaves undisturbed
a policy first advertised openly and unequivocally as a 'total and complete
shutdown of Muslims entering the United States' because the policy now
masquerades behind a façade of national-security concerns").

33. 508 U.S. 520 at 547, 558–59, 563, 577–78.

34. See Richard A. Vazquez, *The Practice of Polygamy: Legitimate Free
Exercise of Religion or Legitimate Public Menace? Revisiting* Reynolds *in Light
of Modern Constitutional Jurisprudence*, 5 N.Y.U. J. Legis & Pub. Pol'y 225,
230, 252 (2001).

35. Watson v. Jones, 80 U.S. 679, 727 (1871). These principles apply to
employment decisions of individuals who work as ministerial educators for
religious institutions but not to facilities managers, technology teachers, and
food service directors. See Hosanna-Tabor Evangelical Lutheran Church
and School v. EEOC, 565 U.S. 171 (2012) and Ira C. Lupu and Robert W.
Tuttle, *The Mystery of Unanimity in* Hosanna-Tabor Evangelical Lutheran
Church and School v. EEOC, 20 Lewis and Clark L. Rev. 1265, 1284
(2017) ("If civil courts were free to invalidate decisions made by religious
authorities under these circumstances, the courts would be substituting the
judgment of the state for that of the religious community with respect to the
role and content of ministry"). *Hosanna-Tabor* involved a claim by a fifth-
grade teacher, who had been ordained as a minister in her faith, that she had
been discriminated against on account of her disability. The Court unanimously held that it violates free exercise of religion for the government to

hold a religious institution liable for the choices it makes as to who will be its ministers. The difficulty is that this would seemingly mean that a religion could exempt itself from all discrimination laws by ordaining all of its employees as ministers.

36. Mark E. Chopko and Michael F. Moses, *Freedom to Be Church: Confronting Challenges to the Right of Church Autonomy*, 3 GEO. J.L. & PUB. POL'Y 388 (2005). See also Douglas Laycock, *The Things That Are Not Caeser's: Religious Organizations as a Check on the Authoritarian Pretensions of the State: Church Autonomy Revisited*, 7 GEO J.L. & PUB. POL'Y 253, 254 ("The essence of church autonomy is that the . . . church should be run by duly constituted [church] authorities and not by legislators, administrative agencies, labor unions, disgruntled lay people, or other actors lacking authority under church law").

37. See Heffron v. International Soc'y for Krishna Consciousness, Inc. 452 U.S. 640 (1981).

38. Marci Hamilton, GOD VS. THE GAVEL: RELIGION AND THE RULE OF LAW (2005), at 7; see also Marci Hamilton, *The Waterloo for the So-Called Church Autonomy Theory: Widespread Clergy Abuse and Institutional Cover-Up*, 29 CARDOZO L. REV. 225 (2007). Her view is that "most laws should govern religious conduct, with the only exception when the legislature has determined that immunizing religious conduct is consistent with public welfare, health, and safety. Hamilton, GOD VS. THE GAVEL, at 8.

39. Moreover, in the Establishment Clause context, institutions that were seeking access to aid would present themselves as non-religious. But in the Free Exercise context, individuals would present themselves as religious to get an exemption from a law. The line-drawing in theory might be equally problematic, but in realize the issue of distinguishing religious and non-religious beliefs arises only in free exercise cases.

40. Madison, Memorial and Remonstrance against Religious Assessments in 2 THE WRITINGS OF JAMES MADISON 183–91 (G. Hunt ed., 1901); Note, *Toward a Constitutional Definition of Religion*, 91 HARV. L. REV. 1056, 1060 n.26 (1978).

41. 380 U.S. 163, 164–66 (1965).

42. 398 U.S. 333, 339 (1970).

43. There is a rich literature focusing on the question of the definition of religion. See, e.g., Stanley Ingber, *Religion or Ideology: A Needed Clarification of the Religion Clauses*, 41 STAN. L. REV. 233 (1989); Jesse Choper,

Defining "Religion" in the First Amendment, 1982 U. ILL. L. REV. 579; Note, *Toward a Constitutional Definition of Religion,* 91 HARV. L. REV. 1056 (1978).

44. George C. Freeman, *The Misguided Search for the Constitutional Definition of "Religion,"* 71 GEO. L.J. 1519, 1548 (1983).

45. See "Religion Based on Sex Gets a Judicial Review," N.Y. TIMES (May 1, 1990), Section A, Page 17, at https://www.nytimes.com/1990/05/02/us/religion-based-on-sex-gets-a-judicial-review.html, and Steve Padilla, *"High Priestess," Husband Sentenced for Prostitution,* L.A. TIMES (Sep. 23, 1989) at https://www.latimes.com/archives/la-xpm-1989-09-23-me-547-story.html ("Prosecutors also noted Mary Ellen Tracy's unorthodox vestments: fishnet stockings, black spiked heels, and a strapless dress studded with red sequins").

46. Ira C. Lupu, *Where Rights Begin: The Problem of Burdens on the Free Exercise of Religion,* 102 HARV. L. REV. 933, 947 (1989). Note also Bruce Friedrich, *The Church of Animal Liberation: Animal Rights as "Religion" under the Free Exercise Clause,* 21 ANIMAL L. REV. 65 (2014) (arguing that animal liberation activists might receive broader protections against government if they incorporated a "Church of Animal Liberation" and claimed free exercise protections).

47. Mozert v. Hawkins County Pub. Schools, 827 F.2d 1058 (6th Cir. 1987) at 1070; Luke v. Williams, No. CV 09-CV-307-MO, 2010 U.S. Dist. LEXIS 123752 (D. Or. Nov. 19, 2010). See also Ira C. Lupu and Robert W. Tuttle, *The Forms and Limits of Religious Accommodation: The Case of RLUIPA,* 3 CARDOZO L. REV. 1907, 1931–32 (2011).

48. West Virginia State Board of Education v. Barnette, 319 U.S. 624, 642 (1943) (Jackson, J.).

49. As Lupu notes, if the Court of Appeals judges in *Mozert* were instead to have upheld the district court's decision permitting the parents to withdraw their children on condition that the parents provide adequate alternative reading instruction, the result would have raised "a host of questions that cannot possibly be answered with confidence. How many children will be removed from the reading program? How will the number change over time? How will it be distributed across the grades? Of what quality will the alternative instruction be, and how will it compare with what the state would have provided? What impact will the departure of those children who do not participate in the reading curriculum have on

those who remain?" Ira C. Lupu, *Where Rights Begin: The Problem of Burdens on the Free Exercise of Religion*, 102 HARV. L. REV. 933, 951 (1989).

50. 450 U.S. 707 (1981).

51. See William P. Marshall, *The Case against the Constitutionally Compelled Free Exercise Exemption*, 40 CASE W. RES. L. REV. 357, 392 (1989) and Christopher L. Eisgruber and Lawrence G. Sager, *Why the Religious Freedom Restoration Act Is Unconstitutional*, 69 N.Y.U. L. REV. 437, 453–54 (1994) ("RFRA's compelling state interest test privileges religious believers by giving them an ill-defined and potentially sweeping right to claim exemption from generally applicable laws, while comparably serious secular commitments—such as those flowing from parental obligation, philosophical conviction, or lifelong cultural practice—receive no such legal solicitude").

52. Ira Lupu, *Where Rights Begin: The Problem of Burdens on the Free Exercise of Religion*, 102 HARV. L. REV. 933, 947fn61 (1989); see Thomas v. Review Bd. of the Ind. Employment Sec. Div., 450 U.S. 707, 720 (1981) (Rehnquist, J., dissenting); Sherbert v. Verner, 374 U.S. 398, 415 (Stewart, J., concurring). See also Philip Kurland, *Of Church and State and the Supreme Court*, 29 U. CHI. L. REV. 1, 96 (1961).

53. John Witte, Jr., RELIGION AND THE AMERICAN CONSTITUTIONAL EXPERIMENT (2nd. ed. 2005), 250.

54. Brian Leiter, WHY TOLERATE RELIGION 33 (2013). See also Lauren Sudeall Lucas, *The Free Exercise of Religious Identity*, 64 UCLA L. REV. 54 (2017) (arguing that law should protect the individual's right to define and pursue one's own identity within a more limited, internal sphere, but that law, and not identity, should govern relationships among individuals and groups in society). See also Christopher L. Eisgruber and Lawrence G. Sager, RELIGIOUS FREEDOM AND THE CONSTITUTION 6 (2007) (noting that the concept of "Equal Liberty . . . denies that religion is a constitutional anomaly, a category of human experience that demands special benefits and/or necessitates special restrictions"). Compare Christopher C. Lund, *Religion Is Special Enough*, 103 VIRGINIA L. REV. 481 (2017) (arguing that religious freedom serves the same kinds of values as other rights and should be treated as one important liberty within the pantheon of human freedoms).

55. See Kathleen A. Brady, THE DISTINCTIVENESS OF RELIGION IN AMERICAN LAW: RETHINKING RELIGION CLAUSE JURISPRUDENCE 197 (2015).

56. See Brian Leiter, WHY TOLERATE RELIGION 1–3, 64–66 (2013), referring to the Canadian Supreme Court case Multani v. Commission scolaire Marguerite-Bourgeoys, 2006 SCC 6 (2006) (affirming the right of a Sikh child to carry his ceremonial knife in school).

57. Ira C. Lupu, *Hobby Lobby and the Dubious Enterprise of Religious Exemptions*, 38 HARV. J.L. & GENDER 35, 72–73 (2015).

58. See Ira C. Lupu, *The Failure of RFRA*, 20 U. ARK. LITTLE ROCK L.J. 575 (1998).

59. See Christopher C. Lund, *Religious Liberty after Gonzales: A Look at State RFRAs*, 55 S.D. L. REV. 466 (2010).

60. Ira C. Lupu and Robert W. Tuttle, *The Forms and Limits of Religious Accommodation: The Case of RLUIPA*, 32 CARDOZO L. REV. 1907, 1908 (2011); see also Ira C. Lupu and Robert W. Tuttle, SECULAR GOVERNMENT, RELIGIOUS PEOPLE (2014).

61. Douglas NeJaime and Reva B. Siegel, *Conscience Wars: Complicity-Based Conscience Claims in Religion and Politics*, 124 YALE L.J. 2516, 2520 (2015).

62. Alex J. Luchenitser, *A New Era of Inequality? Hobby Lobby and Religious Exemptions from Anti-Discrimination Laws*, 9 HARV. L & POL'Y REV. 63, 87 (2015). Professor Oleske proposes an approach that would require the Court to provide an exemption if the government only has a de minimis interest in denying the exemption and if the exemption is easily provided. See James M. Oleske, *A Regrettable Invitation to "Constitutional Resistance," Renewed Confusion over Religious Exemptions, and the Future of Free Exercise*, 20 LEWIS & CLARK L. REV. 1317, 1361 (2017).

63. Holt v. Hobbs, 135 S. Ct. 853 (2015).

64. The Court upheld the right of a Muslim prisoner to have a half-inch beard in Holt v. Hobbs, 135 U.S. 853 (2015), using the strict scrutiny standard that was required under RLUIPA. But it is clear from the Court's assessment of the government's rationale for the prohibition that the Court could have just as easily concluded that the regulation was not neutral and of general applicability, and thus struck it down using the same approach adopted by Justice Kennedy in *Lyng*.

65. An important related issue arises when we consider the question of whether a religious hospital that serves not only members of a church but also the general public can be required to abide by laws regarding the standard of care that must be provided. The issue is especially sensitive

when we consider the role of Catholic hospitals in the structure of American health care. Catholic health systems constitute the largest group of not-for-profit health care providers in the United States (see Catholic Health Association of the United States https://www.chausa.org/about/about/facts-statistics), and they follow the Ethical and Religious Directives (ERDs) for Catholic Health Care Services issued by the United States Conference of Catholic Bishops. These ERDs substantially constrain care and information provided to patients by prohibiting otherwise standardized health care such as contraception, tubal-ligation, vasectomy, abortion, assisted reproductive technology, and certain modalities for end-of-life care. There actually are three questions. First, in the absence of legal regulation may such hospitals refuse to provide care that conflicts with its religious beliefs? The answer is clearly yes; if no law imposes a contrary duty, the hospital can make its own choices. Second, can a law—whether it is a statute or tort law—require that all hospitals provide certain medical coverage even if it violates the religious beliefs of the hospital? Under the position we advocate in this chapter, there is no free exercise exemption for any business from a neutral law of general applicability. This would be true for hospitals and medical care providers as well. Third, can a government institution, such as a university, affiliate with a hospital that refuses to provide certain medical services on account of the hospital's religious affiliation? We see such an affiliation as violating the Establishment Clause as then the government would be denying medical care on account of religion.

66. See Lauren Sidney Flicker, *Religious Employers and Exceptions to Mandated Coverage of Contraceptives*, 15 AMA JOURNAL OF ETHICS 220 (2013), and Laurie Goodstein, *Bishops Reject White House's New Plan on Contraception*, N.Y. TIMES (Feb. 11, 2012), at https://www.nytimes.com/2012/02/12/us/catholic-bishops-criticize-new-contraception-proposal.html.

67. 573 U.S. 682, 706–7, 728, 731, 739–40, 754, 760–61, 770–72 (2014) (internal citations omitted).

68. Erwin Chemerinsky and Michele Goodwin, *Religion Is Not a Basis for Harming Others*, 104 GEORGETOWN L.J. 1111, 1134 (2016).

69. Stormans, Inc. v. Wiesman, 794 F.3d 1064 (9th Cir. 2015).

70. Paul A. Offit, BAD FAITH: WHEN RELIGIOUS BELIEF UNDERMINES MODERN MEDICINE (2015) and Erwin Chemerinsky and Michele Goodwin, *Religion Is Not a Basis for Harming Others*, 104 GEORGETOWN L.J. 1111, 1113–6 (2016); Benitez v. N. Coast Women's Care Med. Grp., 106 Cal. App. 4th 978,

988–9 (2003) (holding that ERISA did not preempt a patient's claims against her doctors alleging they refused to provide additional fertility treatments because of her sexual orientation); Erwin Chemerinsky and Michele Goodwin, *Compulsory Vaccination Laws Are Constitutional*, 110 Nw. U. L. Rev. 589 (2016), Jacobson v. Massachusetts, 197 U.S. 11 (1905) (upholding compulsory vaccination laws when they are "necessary for the public health or the public safety"), and Zucht v. King, 260 U.S. 174 (1922) (upholding childhood vaccination requirements for entrance to public schools).

71. Benjamin Weiser and Margot Sanger-Katz, Judge Voids Trump-Backed 'Conscience Rule' for Health Workers, N.Y. Times, Nov.6, 2019, at https://www.nytimes.com/2019/11/06/upshot/trump-conscience-rule-overturned.html.

72. 930 F.3d 543 (3d Cir. 2019).

73. 930 F.3d 543 (3d Cir. 2019).

74. See Obergefell v. Hodges, 135 S. Ct. 2071 (2015) (holding that the Fourteenth Amendment requires states to license and recognize same-sex marriage); Richard Wolf, *Gay Marriage Victory at Supreme Court Triggering Backlash*, USA Today (May 29, 2016), at https://www.usatoday.com/story/news/politics/2016/05/29/gay-lesbian-transgender-religious-exemption-supreme-court-north-carolina/84908172/.

75. James M. Oleske, Jr., *The Evolution of Accommodation: Comparing the Unequal Treatment of Religious Objections to Interracial and Same-Sex Marriages*, 50 Harv. C.R.-C.L. L. Rev. 99, 101–2 (2015), and citations contained therein.

76. Douglas Laycock, *Tax Exemptions for Racially Discriminatory Schools*, 60 Tex. L. Rev. 259, 263 (1982).

77. Douglas Laycock, *Afterward*, in Same-Sex Marriage and Religious Liberty: Emerging Conflicts (Douglas Laycock et al. eds., 2008), 201; this seeming reversal was noted by Oleske, *The Evolution of Accommodation*, 129.

78. As Chai Feldman put it, "If I am denied a job, an apartment, a room at a hotel, a table at a restaurant, or a procedure by a doctor because I am a lesbian, that is a deep, intense, and tangible hurt. That hurt is not alleviated because I might be able to go down the street and get a job, an apartment, a hotel room, a restaurant table, or a medical procedure from someone else. . . . The assault to my dignity and my sense of safety in the world occurs when the initial denial happens." Chai R. Feldblum, *Moral*

Conflict and Conflicting Liberties, in SAME-SEX MARRIAGE AND RELIGIOUS LIBERTY: EMERGING CONFLICTS (Douglas Laycock et al. eds., 2008), 153.

79. Chris Joyner, *Georgia Mayor under Fire for Alleged Remarks about Black Job Candidate*, ATLANTA JOURNAL-CONSTITUTION (May 6, 2019), at https://www.ajc.com/news/local-govt--politics/georgia-mayor-under-fire-for-alleged-remarks-about-black-job-candidate/Qr403ZLnF5VuB8CzpngLjP/?fbclid=IwARof8pcGjO7Ehg33Xl9Qz-FKnjfrsa8Cb-BBO5fvYu27-8d36H1MHPA4UBE.

80. Robin Fretwell Wilson, *The Calculus of Accommodation: Contraception, Abortion, Same-Sex Marriage, and Other Clashes between Religion and the State*, 53 B.C. L. REV. 1417, 1432 (2012).

81. Note, for example, the Manhattan Declaration: A Call of Christian Conscience, the 2009 manifesto of conservative Christian principles set forth by Princeton Professor Robert George and former Watergate conspirator Chuck Colson. Endorsed by Catholic and evangelical Protestant leaders as well as conservative political activists, it called on Christians to unite across denominational lines to support the sanctity of life, the dignity of marriage as between a husband and a wife, and the freedom of religion. They seek to build a movement of millions of individuals, who among other things would be committed to advocating religious-based exemptions to laws involving access to certain health care procedures and same-sex marriage. Manhattan Declaration: A Call of Christian Conscience, Manhattan Declaration (Nov. 2009), http://manhattandeclaration.org/man_dec_resources/Manhattan_Declaration_full_text.pdf and List of Religious & Organizational Leaders Signatories, Manhattan Declaration, http://manhattandeclaration.org/man_dec_resources/list_of_religious_leaders.pdf. See Douglas NeJaime and Reva B. Siegel, *Conscience Wars: Complicity-Based Conscience Claims in Religion and Politics*, 124 YALE L.J. 2516, 2542–53 (2015).

82. Douglas NeJaime and Reva B. Siegel, *Conscience Wars: Complicity-Based Conscience Claims in Religion and Politics*, 124 YALE L.J. 2516 (2015). See also Amy J. Sepinwall, *Conscience and Complicity: Assessing Pleas for Religious Exemptions in Hobby Lobby's Wake*, 82 U. CHI. L. REV. 1897, 1915–23 (2015) (noting that "complicity" assumes more direct participation, as opposed to remote facilitation, in the immoral actions of others).

83. For examples of such claims see Odgaard v. Iowa Civil Rights Comm'n, No. CV046451 (Iowa Dist. Ct. Apr. 3, 2014); Elane Photography, 309 P.3d 53; Complaint, Arlene's Flowers, Inc. v. Ferguson, No. 13-2-01898-2

(Wash. Super. Ct. Aug. 1, 2013); Mullins v. Masterpiece Cakeshop, Inc., No. CR2013-0008 (Colo. Admin. Ct. Dec. 6, 2013).

84. Elane Photography, LLC v. Willock, 309 P.3d. 53, 64, 67-68 (N.M. 2013). The U.S. Supreme Court refused to hear an appeal from this case; see Elane Photography, LLC v. Willock, 572 U.S. 1046 (2014).

85. State v. Arlene's Flowers, Inc., 187 Wn.2d. 804, 826, 829 (2017).

86. Masterpiece Cakeshop, Ltd. v. Colorado Civil Rights Commission, 138 S.Ct. 1719 (2018).

87. Mullins v. Masterpiece Cakeshop, Inc., No. CR2013-0008, slip op. at 3 (Colo. Admin. Ct. Dec. 6, 2013).

88. 138 S.Ct. 1719, 1721–22, 1723–24, 1729–30, 1733.

89. It may be asked whether our objections to the free exercise rights in these cases should also extend to the free speech (compelled speech) arguments. If people cannot escape their civic obligations by invoking free exercise claims why should they escape their obligations by invoking free speech claims? The free/compelled speech arguments would take longer to elaborate than we should spend in a treatment of the Religion Clauses, but it would focus on the difference between justifying discriminatory activity on grounds of religious belief versus not discriminating against anyone but merely refusing to write certain messages for anyone.

90. 2019 U.S. App. LEXIS 25320.

91. Katzenbach v. McClung, 389 U.S. 374 (1965) (upholding Title II of the 1964 Civil Rights Act, which prohibits race discrimination by hotels and restaurants).

92. Brush & Nib Studios v. City of Phoenix, 2019 Ariz. LEXIS 280.

93. Ira C. Lupu and Robert W. Tuttle, *The Forms and Limits of Religious Accommodation: The Case of RLUIPA*, 32 CARDOZO L. REV. 1907, 1909 (2011).

94. Dalia Fahmy, *Americans Are Far More Religious than Adults in Other Wealthy Nations*, PEWRESEARCH.COM (July 31, 2018), https://www.pewresearch.org/fact-tank/2018/07/31/americans-are-far-more-religious-than-adults-in-other-wealthy-nations/.

95. *Id.*

96. Fulton v. City of Philadelphia, 922 F.3d 140 (3rd Cir. 2019), cert. granted, 139 S.Ct. (2020).

97. See Linda Greenhouse, *Religious Crusaders at the Supreme Court's Gates*, N.Y. TIMES (Sept. 12, 2019), at https://www.nytimes.com/2019/09/12/opinion/supreme-court-religion.html.

1. See Douglas Laycock, *Religious Liberty as Liberty*, 7 J. CONTEMPORARY LEGAL ISSUES 313 (1996) ("the core point . . . is that the government does not take positions on religious questions—not in its daily administration, not in its laws, and not in its Constitution either").

2. *Id.* at 314.

3. Indeed, Justice Scalia said this directly in his dissent in McCreary County, Kentucky v. ACLU of Kentucky, 545 U.S. 844, 894 (2005), which declared unconstitutional the posting of the Ten Commandments in government buildings: "The three most popular religions in the United States, Christianity, Judaism, and Islam—which combined account for 97.7% of all believers—are monotheistic. . . . All of them, moreover (Islam included), believe that the Ten Commandments were given by God to Moses, and are divine prescriptions for a virtuous life. Publicly honoring the Ten Commandments is thus indistinguishable, insofar as discriminating against other religions is concerned, from publicly honoring God. Both practices are recognized across such a broad and diverse range of the population—from Christians to Muslims—that they cannot be reasonably understood as a government endorsement of a particular religious viewpoint."

4. School District of Abington Township v. Schempp, 374 U.S. 203, 225–6 (1963).

5. Lynch v. Donnelly, 465 U.S. 668 (1984).

6. Stone v. Graham, 449 U.S. 39 (1980).

7. Epperson v. Arkansas, 393 U.S. 97 (1968).

8. Abington School District v. Schempp, 374 U.S. 203 (1963).

9. Engel v. Vitale, 370 U.S. 421 (1962).

10. Illinois ex rel. McCollum v. Board of Education, 333 U.S. 203 (1948).

11. Consider, for example, the case of Rajneeshpuram, a community in Wasco County, Oregon, briefly incorporated as a city in the 1980s, which was populated with Rajneeshees, followers of the spiritual teacher Rajneesh. See *Rajneeshees in Oregon: An Untold History*, OREGONLIVE.COM, https://www.oregonlive.com/rajneesh/page/post.html.

12. Wallace v. Jaffree, 472 U.S. 38 (1985) (declaring unconstitutional a state law requiring schools begin each day with a moment of silent prayer).

13. Laycock's voluminous writings have been recently collected in an impressive five-volume set; see Douglas Laycock, RELIGIOUS LIBERTY (set of 5 volumes) (2018). Not that it matters, but he has explained in deeply personal ways that he comes to these questions as a person who considers himself a child of the Enlightenment and an agnostic. See Douglas Laycock, *Religious Liberty as Liberty*, 7 J. CONTEM. L. ISSUES 313, 352–56 (1996) (ending his discussion by saying that his "goal is to enable people on both sides of such divides to live together in peace and equality and without surrender of religious autonomy").

14. Laycock, *Religious Liberty as Liberty*, 313–14, 317, 319.

15. *Id.* at 331.

16. 380 U.S. 163 (1965) (holding that the exemption from the military draft for conscientious objectors could not be reserved only for those professing conformity with the moral directives of a supreme being, but also for those whose views on war derived from a "sincere and meaningful belief which occupies in the life of its possessor a place parallel to that filled by the God of those" who had routinely gotten the exemption).

17. 398 U.S. 333 (1970) (holding that conscientious objector status applies to "all those whose consciences, spurred by deeply held moral, ethical, or religious beliefs, would give them no rest or peace if they allowed themselves to become a part of an instrument of war").

18. Laycock, *Religious Liberty as Liberty*, 347.

19. *Id.* at 332–33.

20. *Id.* at 349.

21. See Brief of Douglas Laycock et al. as Amici Curiae in Support of Petitioners, *Obergefell v. Hodges*, 135 S. Ct. 2584 (2015) (No. 14–556), 2015 WL 1048450.

22. Douglas Laycock, *The Campaign against Religious Liberty*, in THE RISE OF CORPORATE RELIGIOUS LIBERTY 231 (Micah Schwartman, Chad Flanders, and Zoe Robinson eds. 2016), 243–46.

23. *Id.* at 254–55.

24. But this should not be seen as giving religious entities exemptions from all anti-discrimination laws. In October Term 2019, the Supreme Court has two cases as to whether a religious school is exempt from employment discrimination laws for its teachers who are not ordained as clergy. Our Lady of Guadalupe School v. Morrissey Beru, 769 Fed.Appx. 460 (9th Cir. 2019); St. James School v. Biel, 911 F.3d 603

NOTES

(9ᵗʰ Cir. 2018). In light of our analysis in Chapter 4, we believe that the anti-discrimination laws should be applied to protect these teachers. The alternative is to give religious institutions the right to discriminate on the basis of race, sex, religion, sexual orientation, disability and other prohibited grounds. Our position is that anti-discrimination statutes are neutral laws of general applicability under *Employment Division v. Smith*. At the very least, stopping discrimination should be deemed a compelling government interest.

25. 42 U.S.C. SECTION 2000e-1(a) (2012) and Center for American Progress Action Fund, *A State-by-State Examination of Nondiscrimination Laws and Policies* 3–4 (2012), https://www.americanprogress.org/wp-content/uploads/issues/2012/06/pdf/state_nondiscrimination.pdf.

26. See Robin Fretwell Wilson, Marriage of Necessity: Same-Sex Marriage and Religious Liberty Protections, 64 Case W. Reserve L. Rev. 1161 (2014).

27. From James Madison to Edward Livingston, July 10, 1822, available at the National Archives' Founders Online, https://founders.archives.gov/documents/Madison/04-02-02-0471.

Index

· · ·

Page references to notes are indicated by *n*'s.

For the benefit of digital users, indexed terms that span two pages (e.g., 52–53) may, on occasion, appear on only one of those pages.